THE WRECK OF THE CIRCUS SHIP *ROYAL TAR*

TRAGEDY IN PENOBSCOT BAY

JANE PARKS GARDNER

THE History PRESS

Published by The History Press
An imprint of Arcadia Publishing
Charleston, SC
www.historypress.com

Cover image: Nova Scotia Archives, 6016 University Avenue, Halifax, Nova Scotia, Canada B3H 1W4.

First published 2025

Manufactured in the United States

ISBN 9781467158510

Library of Congress Control Number: 2025933741

Nearly all those who perished were strangers in a strange land,
far from their home and kindred.

—Henry H. Fuller, manager of Fuller's Menagerie,
October 29, 1836

This book is dedicated to my parents, Roger H. Parks and Joan C. Parks.
In loving memory of my father, whose love and wisdom continue to guide me.
And to my mother, because strong women raise strong daughters.

CONTENTS

ACKNOWLEDGEMENTS

"Write a book," they said. "It'll be fun," they promised. "Easy peasy!"

It has been an adventure, though not exactly easy peasy (okay, no one actually said that). Writing a book is often a lonely, solitary endeavor, but without the support of those around you, it would be an infinitely more daunting task. I am fortunate to have a wonderful group of people on "Team Jane" who stood by me throughout this process, and I am deeply grateful to each and every one of you.

A very warm thank-you to a few dear friends: to Jane Willan, who has been my friend for over two decades and has always encouraged my writing projects; to Jeff Belanger, who helped me navigate much of this process; and to Scott and LeAnn Rutherford, who provided invaluable nautical insights and many laughs.

Thank you to Mike Kinsella at Arcadia Publishing, who believed in this project as much as I did. Thank you to Hilary Parrish at The History Press and Shannon Scott at Sage Editing for their helpful editorial reviews.

And to my two favorite people on the planet, my sons, Jesse and Emmett, who brainstormed with me, edited for me, encouraged me every step of the way, and always responded to every single random text I sent about elephants—thank you from the bottom of my heart.

A very special thank-you to the staff at the following locations who provided research and archival materials:

- Boston Public Library, Boston, Massachusetts
- Izaak Walton Killam Memorial Library, Yarmouth, Nova Scotia

- Vinalhaven Historical Society, Vinalhaven, Maine, for their help and willingness to email images when I couldn't get a ferry ticket in time
- Mia Sigler at Brown Research Library, Portland, Maine, for her assistance with the microfiche machine and research materials
- Melrose Public Library, Melrose, Massachusetts
- Penobscot Marine Museum, Searsport, Maine
- Peter Dahlen with Sebago Brewing Company, Gorham, Maine, who let me use their art and gave me a couple cans of *Royal Tar* Imperial Stout
- The office staff and groundskeepers at Fernhill Cemetery, Saint John, New Brunswick, who helped me find Captain Reed's grave
- The staff at Peavy Memorial Library, Eastport, Maine, who listened to my stories on a hot July day
- Irish Canadian Cultural Association of New Brunswick, Saint John Chapter
- Audrey Farch of the Reg Erhardt Library, Southern Alberta Institute of Technology

PROLOGUE

BOSTON, MASSACHUSETTS, MAY 13, 1831

Slowly, gently, and with great skill, the ship *Neponset* coasted into the docks at Boston Harbor. After weeks at sea, traveling all the way from Calcutta (now Kolkata in West Bengal, India), the passengers were weary and grateful to see land. Perhaps none more so than two very special passengers: a rhinoceros and an Asian elephant.

The elephant, still a youngster at nine years old, was weak from the long voyage. Scarred from jungle fights, thin and disoriented, the mighty animal took tentative steps off the gangplank and onto the firm land of New England. His intelligent eyes surveyed his new home, so different from the jungle he had left not long ago. Alone, scared, and exhausted, the elephant took another tentative step on land. This was the noble Mogul's new home.

INTRODUCTION

THIS IS A STORY...

This is a story of a tragedy. In October 1836, a ship carrying ninety-three passengers and crew, as well as a circus menagerie, wax museum, and brass band, caught fire and sank in the cold, dark waters of Penobscot Bay off the coast of Maine. A total of thirty-three passengers, crew, and all the animals, both caged and free, perished that fateful day.

It is also a story about a ship. The *Royal Tar*, a sidewheel steamship, made her maiden voyage in the summer of 1836. Built of Canadian lumber in the docks near Saint John, New Brunswick, she was fast and capable. Her task was to make weekly trips from Saint John to Portland, with a stop in Eastport, Maine. She was a ferry, of sorts, transporting people, goods, and the occasional elephant up and down the East Coast. Some records indicate she was the first of her kind and as luxurious as the finest hotel, and as history would show, she was not the last.

This is a story about people and human nature. Nothing tests an individual or a group more than an emergency, where quick thinking, wits, and the will to live must kick into gear instantaneously to survive. There were accidents, and mistakes were made. Heroes sprang into action that cold October afternoon, in some cases literally serving as lifelines for others. And there were cowards who thought only of themselves.

It is a story about a traveling circus. Mogul the elephant, two camels, a gnu (wildebeest), exotic snakes, a gentle Bengal tiger, and two lionesses had been uprooted from their distant homes and placed into involuntary servitude by circus showmen. They traveled by night, from Boston through the Canadian provinces, performing their routines or simply idling in their cages. These animals met their fate in the cold ocean waters of Penobscot Bay.

And it is a story of an era. A time when passage on a ship from Saint John, New Brunswick, to Portland, Maine, cost eight dollars. When newspapers were filled with stories of shipwrecks and the dangers of the high seas. It was a time of relative prosperity, between the economic crises of 1819 and 1837, a time when people had an extra twenty-five cents to take their families to see the traveling circus. A time when immigrants from Ireland came to Canada and the United States, not because of the potato famine (that was a few years to come) but to chase the dream of a brighter future. A time when boats were powered by boilers, when lifejackets were nonexistent, and when weight and passenger limits on vessels were rudimentary. A time when communication on ships, between the firemen below and the captain, was limited to a series of bells or tubes. A time without GPS or weather reports.

It is the story of the *Royal Tar*.

CHAPTER 1

THE BOAT

In the 1830s, traveling over land from New Brunswick to New England could take several days or even longer due to the uncertainty and obstacles of the route. Consequently, travel by water became the most practical option. Coastal merchants in New Brunswick and Nova Scotia, motivated by trade opportunities, enlisted timber harvesters and shipbuilders to construct ships and schooners for both travel and commerce. These efforts spurred economic growth in the region, fostering a thriving maritime industry. Wooden sailboats, dependent on wind and weather, frequently navigated this well-trodden route. It was often taken by European immigrants seeking a new life in the United States or by laborers or tradesmen moving between jobs. Ships also transported lumber and various goods and occasionally even entertainment troupes. However, for those looking to save time, steamships offered a quicker alternative. The journey from Saint John, New Brunswick, to Portland, Maine, by steamship took only a few days, making it a surprisingly fast option.

Shipbuilding

Shipbuilding was a significant industry in the late 1700s to early 1800s, and New Brunswick's forests of spruce, white pine, and birch provided the perfect lumber for constructing steamships and schooners. These vessels were integral to the maritime activities of the time, reflecting the region's resources and shipbuilding expertise. In the early 1830s, a group of investors sought to capitalize on the growing steam-powered technology by building a steamship to connect coastal New Brunswick to New England. Investors put up a total of $40,000—equivalent to $1.4 million in 2024 dollars—to build this pioneer steamship. Half of the venture was supported by John Hammond, while the other half was funded by Daniel McLaughlin and Mackay Brothers & Co. The boat was built from Canadian timber in a boatyard owned by William and Isaac Olive in Carleton, New Brunswick, on the Saint John River. This substantial investment not only boosted the local economy by creating jobs in the shipbuilding industry, but it also stimulated related sectors such as timber, transportation, and trade. The project, and others like it, positioned New Brunswick as a key player in the North American shipbuilding industry, contributing to the region's economic growth and development.

The boat was a marvel of its time—a steam-powered schooner, a hybrid with two masts and a boiler and engine below deck. Records indicate that at the stern of the boat, there was a canvas-covered pavilion, or something like a tent. The area midship was open. Closer to the bow were two smokestacks with a mast between them. The specs of the boat were given in *The New Brunswick Magazine*:

- 400 tons burthen—this is an estimated tonnage (the capacity of the ship) based on the length and the measurement of the widest spot on the ship (the beam)
- 146-foot keel
- 160 feet on deck
- 24-foot beam

At the time, most of the transoceanic ships being built were sailing vessels. Some found steam-powered boats less than ideal, as the boiler technology was often unreliable and could be dangerous. Ships that traveled coastal routes began to embrace steam technology, but for a while, sails were still used as a reliable backup. One such case when the sails might prove to be more useful was when a ship had to fight the tides. Early steam engines were often not powerful enough to do so. While the primary propulsion came from the paddle wheels, the masts and sails provided additional power and stability when required.

This ship built at the Olives' boatyard was considered a large ship for the time and was, according to several sources, outfitted in the finest of ways. The decks were built from local softwood, caulked with oakum, and sealed with tar to make them waterproof. The hull was constructed using sturdy spruce and white pine, chosen for their resilience and buoyancy. Skilled shipwrights carefully shaped each timber, ensuring a perfect fit that would provide the ship with both strength and flexibility to withstand the rough seas.

The boiler, designed to run on wood, was managed by firemen, or stokers, who kept it burning hot. Paddle wheels, deckhouses, and a pilothouse completed the ship's structure. The ship's two large paddle wheels were positioned on either side, powered by the steam engine below deck. These wheels, crafted from reinforced timber and iron, were essential for the vessel's propulsion.

The steam engine in this boat was an adaptation of the beam engine, called the walking beam or vertical beam. Introduced for use in seagoing ships, the walking beam quickly became the most popular engine type for inland waterways and coastal service due to its durability. Characterized by its reinforced iron struts forming a diamond shape supported by wooden

Compound beam engine of the Fall River Line steamer *Puritan* (1891). The steel-framed engine, built by W. & A. Fletcher Co. of Hoboken, New Jersey, was the largest vertical beam (i.e. walking beam) engine ever constructed. Scientific American, *public domain via Wikimedia Commons.*

structures, the walking beam extended above the ship's deck. Its rocking motion resembled walking. Primarily used for paddle-wheel engines in rivers, lakes, and coastal areas, the walking beam was less popular for seagoing vessels. Its popularity was largely because it suited the shallow-draft boats navigating the United States' coastal and inland waterways.

The boilers created steam that turned the axles, moving the paddle wheels. A vessel such as this, intended to travel close to shore along the coast or up a river, would have had paddles that extended only five to six feet into the water. This prevented damage to the paddles, as repairs were costly and resulted in lost time and canceled trips.

No photographs or images of the boat from before her untimely end exist today. The only visual records are paintings created after the ship's tragic fire. Boats at that time were often built without official plans or blueprints. However, based on what is known about two-masted steam-powered schooners, one might imagine her with a main deck featuring cabins for wealthier passengers, a small pilothouse with windows on three sides for a clear view, and two large masts with sails ready to be unfurled if needed.

Passenger accommodations were divided by class. Wealthier passengers enjoyed private cabins on the main deck, each fitted with comfortable beds, fine furnishings, and ample space. These cabins were designed to offer a luxurious journey, with windows providing views of the sea. The main deck

This boat was a wooden-sided two-masted steamship that probably looked similar to the steamer *Mt. Vernon*, pictured here. *Library of Congress.*

also featured a dining area where lavish meals were served, enhancing the experience of the more affluent travelers. Even though the trip took just a few days, it was possible to travel in style.

In contrast, steerage passengers were housed below deck in more cramped and less comfortable conditions. They shared large, communal bunkrooms near the boiler room, where the heat and soot from the machinery made conditions less pleasant. These accommodations consisted of simple wooden bunks stacked in tiers, with limited personal space and minimal amenities. Despite these hardships, many steerage passengers embraced the experience, sharing meals and stories with fellow passengers. The crew had quarters below deck as well, conveniently close to the boilers for the firemen who had to constantly tend to the boiler. Below the main deck were additional cabins and storage spaces for luggage, cargo, and possibly even cages for circus animals. The steam boilers were housed below deck and fueled with wood. Designed to stay close to shore, the ship could carry enough wood to get from port to port. Seagoing ships still relied on sails for their voyages in the early to mid-1800s, as it was impossible to carry enough wood to fuel the boiler for the trip. Coal, while starting to become commonplace in 1836, did not become a more viable fuel for a few more years. Coal was more efficient, as more could be carried on board for longer trips.

Communication on board was a challenge. The firemen kept in touch with the engineer, who monitored the gauges needed to keep the engine running. The engineer, in turn, communicated with the captain on deck, using either a series of tubes or bells. Often, orders were shouted from all corners, making the working part of the boat a noisy and seemingly chaotic place. But everyone knew their job, so ships were well-run methods of transportation.

The steam boiler, a crucial component, required constant attention to prevent overheating—a task that was as dangerous as it was vital. Steamships were a relatively inexpensive way to travel at the time, but they came with their own set of risks. These ships were inherently unsafe. These were wooden vessels carrying huge, heavy iron boilers that could get red-hot. Boilers sometimes exploded as the pressure built up. Another issue was if the boiler ran low on water. One of the most important pieces of safety equipment on a steamship was the boiler sight gauge. The steam boiler pictured here is similar to what would have been on this boat. The gauge would indicate the water levels in the boiler. It was important that the water level not drop too low; if this happened and the boiler wasn't refilled immediately, the boiler itself could become dangerously hot.

The boat was a steam-powered schooner with a wood-fired boiler, similar to this. *Library of Congress.*

In the 1830s, there were no regulations on the number of passengers a boat could carry, a situation that seems unsafe by today's standards. However, practices and safety protocols were different then. It is estimated that there were upward of two hundred people on board for the maiden voyage of this boat. Although this number seems high, several sources provide the same estimate.

There were also no specific regulations regarding the number of lifeboats required on these boats traveling close to shore. Research suggests that there may have been at least four lifeboats on board for the initial voyages, but no one is certain. It is also worth noting that personal flotation devices were not required on such boats at the time. The owners and crew of this boat adhered to all existing regulations, but it appears no additional safety measures were implemented, which was standard practice at the time.

Dangers at Sea

During the 1830s, sea travel was fraught with danger, as evidenced by the frequent reports of shipwrecks and fires that filled the newspapers. The perilous nature of maritime travel at the time added to the sense of dread and uncertainty faced by passengers and crew alike.

For instance, the *Boston Evening Transcript* on October 31, 1836, reported a harrowing account of the *Ariel*, a ship that left New York bound for St. Thomas on August 14, 1836. The *Ariel* was carrying six hundred barrels of flour, twenty-five sugar boilers, fifteen tons of cordage, a half ton of gunpowder, and nine passengers. In the dead of night, the ship caught fire, and despite the valiant efforts of Captain Park to extinguish the flames, the fire raged out of control. The captain, along with the passengers and crew—fourteen people in total—escaped in the longboat, clad only in their nightclothes. They paddled frantically, barely making it half a mile from the ship before it exploded. The survivors drifted at sea for nearly a month, finally reaching land in St. Domingo on September 4, having endured the last four days without water. Remarkably, all survived this terrifying ordeal.

In the same newspaper issue, another tragic event was recounted under the headline "Melancholy Accident." A schooner carrying potatoes and wood set sail from Bath, Maine, bound for Boston. However, the ship was caught in a violent storm seventy miles from Cape Elizabeth. The storm ravaged the ship, and all but one of the crew perished. The sole survivor was the captain, who was eventually rescued after a harrowing ordeal. Among the lost was the captain's nephew, who tragically succumbed to the elements, his body left clinging to the bowsprit of the ship, while the other two crew members were washed overboard.

These accounts, among many others, underscored the treacherous nature of sea travel during this era. The unpredictability of the weather, the vulnerability of ships to fire and storms, and the often inadequate safety measures meant that every voyage carried the potential for disaster.

The *Royal Tar*

The boat owned by Hammond, McLaughlin, and Mackay Brothers & Co. was christened *Royal Tar*. This name is steeped in history. *Tar* is an old term for sailor, while *Royal* refers to the new British king, William IV. Initially not

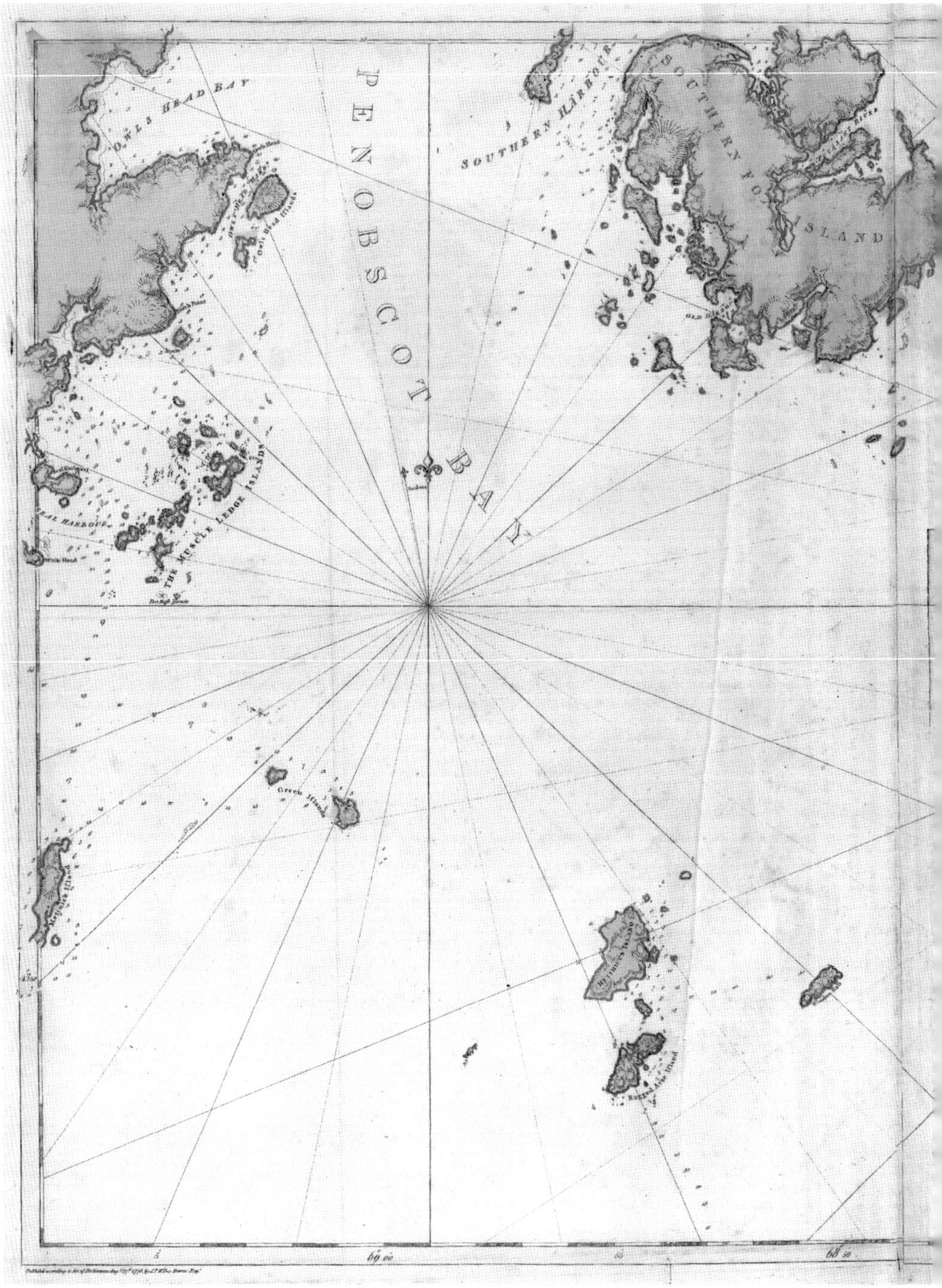
PENOBSCOT BAY
OWLS HEAD BAY
Owls Head Islands
SOUTHERN HARBOUR
SOUTHERN FOX ISLAND
OLD HARBOUR
SEAL HARBOUR
THE MUSCLE LEDGE ISLANDS
Green Islands
Ragged Arse Island
69 00
68 50

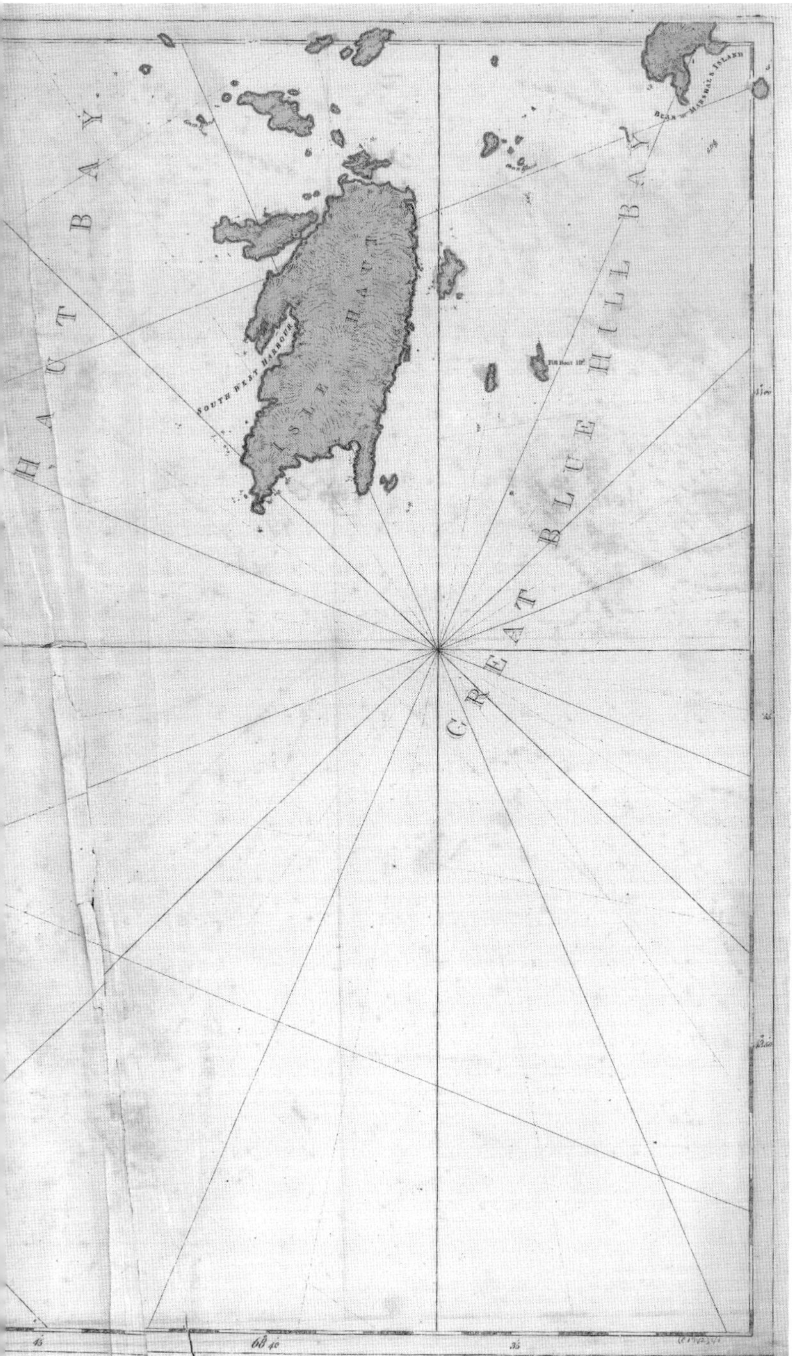

Map of Penobscot Bay from the late 1700s. Captain Reed may have used a map similar to this to navigate the islands in Penobscot Bay on his way to Portland, Maine. After passing through the Fox Island Thoroughfare, the *Royal Tar* sank off the northeastern coast of Southern Fox Island (now Vinalhaven). *Library of Congress.*

in direct line for the throne, William spent his younger years as a sailor, traveling extensively, including to the region now known as Canada. A series of untimely deaths led to his unexpected coronation in 1830 at the age of sixty-four. When the boat launched on its maiden voyage in 1836, toasts were made celebrating "the patriotic and beloved sovereign for whom the '*Royal Tar*' is named—The Sailor King."

The maiden voyage of the *Royal Tar* on Monday, May 2, 1836, was quite the spectacle. The ship's inaugural trip from Partridge Island to Reed's Point took just fifteen minutes, prompting much fanfare and celebration among the owners. To mark the occasion, a lavish luncheon was served to the passengers, courtesy of the owners, with "rivers of sherry and oceans of champagne" flowing freely.

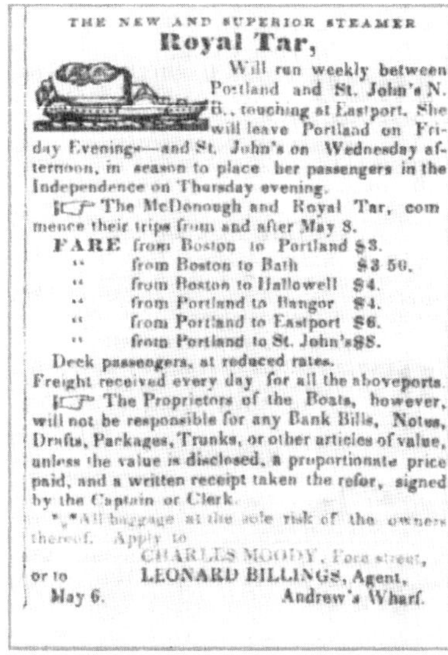

Advertisements for passage on the *Royal Tar* ran alongside other ships in newspapers along the Canadian and New England coasts. Kennebeck Journal, *October 26, 1836, accessed at the Brown Research Library, Portland, Maine.*

The owners opted not to insure the *Royal Tar*. Perhaps they intended to do so in the future, or maybe they had difficulty justifying an increase in the fare to meet the insurance rates. The exact reason is unknown, and it seems foolhardy to those of us living in today's climate. However, in 1836, it was a business decision—one that proved costly in many ways.

After the initial fifteen-minute test run, all that remained was to embark on its intended route. On June 5, 1836, *Royal Tar* made her first trip to Eastport and then to Saint Andrews. The return trip from Eastport to Saint John was completed in less than five hours—a new record for steam navigation at the time!

The *Royal Tar* made trips up and down the Saint John River to Fredericton and also along the coast to Portland. That summer, she was put into regular service, with one trip a week up the river and one trip to Portland and back. Advertisements such as this one ran in newspapers along the New Brunswick and Maine coasts, reaching as far south as Portsmouth, New Hampshire. The word was out that the *Royal Tar* was running weekly trips.

As remarkable as the *Royal Tar* was in terms of engineering and maritime innovation, it was the people aboard her that truly brought her story to life. Each journey carried a mix of passengers and crew—wealthy merchants, hopeful immigrants, hardworking laborers, and curious travelers—all with their own stories and dreams. These individuals, with their personal reasons for travel, their hopes, and their experiences, boarded the *Royal Tar* with caution, knowing that travel was often hazardous. They also boarded with confidence in their captain and his crew. And they boarded with plans for the days ahead after their trip.

CHAPTER 2
THE PEOPLE

Life in the 1830s

Life in New England and eastern Canada during the 1830s was a blend of tradition and change, reflecting the steadfastness of long-established communities and the burgeoning spirit of newcomers. History showed that in general, people forged ahead, literally and in spirit, with a sense of determination and optimism that characterized the era.

In the United States, the spirit of patriotism was palpable, a lingering fervor from the War of 1812 that instilled a sense of national pride. Education was highly valued, with public libraries and newspapers playing crucial roles in spreading knowledge and fostering informed communities. Towns often had one-room schoolhouses where children of all ages learned together, emphasizing reading, writing, arithmetic, and moral lessons. Antislavery sentiment in the North began to take root, reflecting a growing awareness and advocacy for human rights. This period saw significant immigration, with approximately sixty thousand newcomers each year, many from Ireland. They were drawn by the promise of a better life, contributing to the rich tapestry of American society despite facing considerable hardships, far from their homelands.

Agriculture was the backbone of life in many regions, with most people living and working on farms. The urban population was a small minority, dwarfed by the vast numbers of those tilling the land and raising livestock. This rural lifestyle was punctuated by occasional trips to burgeoning towns and cities, where public markets introduced new goods including tomatoes, oranges, ice, and lemons to the general populace. Community events, like fairs, traveling circuses, barn raisings, and church gatherings, were pivotal to social life, offering opportunities for socializing and mutual support. The need for charitable organizations and benevolent institutions grew, addressing the plight of the unemployed poor and immigrants who struggled to find their footing in a new land.

Eastern Canada mirrored much of New England's vibrancy, though it faced unique challenges. The cholera epidemic of 1832 wreaked havoc across Canada and the United States, claiming thousands of lives and instilling a pervasive sense of unease and insecurity. Despite this, the influx of immigrants, particularly from the United Kingdom, continued, with more than twenty-eight thousand arriving in Canada in 1830 alone. The region's public libraries and educational institutions played pivotal roles in integrating these newcomers, providing resources for learning and community building. Social life in Canadian towns often centered on the church, which served as both a place of worship and a community hub.

Fashion in the 1830s was characterized by dramatic silhouettes and elaborate details. Women's clothing featured large sleeves, often supported by ties filled with feathers to create a voluminous effect. The bodice was typically adorned with lace, and skirts required multiple petticoats for fullness, with a bustle tied around the waist to hold the skirt out at the back. Outerwear included shawls, adding another layer of elegance. Lavish use of jewelry was common, with chains draped around the neck, waist, and shoulders or even woven into the hair. Married women wore lace caps indoors and accessorized with hats or bonnets when outside.

Men's fashion emphasized broad shoulders and a narrow waist, often achieved through the cut of their clothing. Greatcoats, with their wide sleeves, were everyday outerwear, complemented by tall hats. Boys typically wore trousers and short jackets, while little girls' outfits mirrored the style of older women, reflecting the fashion trends of the time.

Those traveling at sea in October in eastern Canada and northern New England wore overcoats, shawls, and long sleeves. Although their clothing was similar year-round, citizens added heavier coats and shawls in the cooler months.

Travel in the early 1800s was arduous and slow, yet it was also a time of significant advancements. In the 1790s, New England's roads were often barely passable. Most people traveled on foot, and only a few farmers owned horses and wagons. The primary mode of land transport was horse and buggy, traversing notoriously poor roads. During the spring thaw, snowmelt and rain turned them into quagmires, making travel especially difficult. Freight was commonly hauled by slow-moving oxen. A journey from Boston to New York could take four to six days, even on the best roads. Inland routes were even worse, transforming into treacherous muck or choking dust depending on the weather.

However, around 1790, the "Transportation Revolution" began to transform travel. New England saw the construction of over 3,700 miles of toll roads by 1820 and continued to improve roads into the 1840s. These better roads increased the number of vehicles and stagecoach lines, making travel faster, cheaper, and less dangerous. By the 1830s, a trip from Boston to New York took only a day and a half, and stagecoach routes extended across southern New England and beyond.

This is the typical dress of a woman with modest means in 1836. She may have worn a heavy shawl during the chilly months of autumn. *Los Angeles County Museum of Art, public domain, via Wikimedia Commons.*

The most radical changes came with new transportation technologies: railroads and steamboats. Robert Fulton's invention marked the beginning of steamboat travel in 1807, revolutionizing river transport by allowing vessels to travel against currents and on tighter schedules. While steamboats were prone to fires and boiler explosions, they significantly expanded passenger travel and carried valuable cargo upstream more efficiently than rafts and barges. Steam-powered ships were also added to ocean fleets, providing a new option for shipbuilders up and down the New England and Canada coastlines, though they did not completely replace sailing vessels.

These advancements in transportation reshaped life in New England and eastern Canada. Increased mobility spurred economic growth and cultural exchange, making travel and commerce faster and more reliable. For the passengers on the *Royal Tar*, these changes meant the possibility of new opportunities and adventures. Immigrants, crew members, and circus hands alike benefited from these innovations, symbolizing the era's spirit of progress and the pursuit of a better future.

The Irish Experience in the 1830s

It is well known that life in Ireland in the 1840s was difficult. An estimated one million people perished during the Great Famine of the 1840s, and one to two million more immigrated to Great Britain or North America. North America was a destination for many immigrants from Ireland in the late 1700s and early 1800s. Cities like Boston, New York, and Philadelphia beckoned, growing large, close-knit Irish communities with the influx of immigrants. Drawn initially to opportunities in manufacturing, textiles, and other industries, early settlers set down roots, paving the way for future arrivals. Immigrants of the early to mid-1800s, before the famine in the 1840s, were particularly attracted to these cities because of the strong Irish ties growing there.

In 1836, many of the passengers on the *Royal Tar* were Irish immigrants seeking a better life in North America. It was not unusual for young families to leave Ireland, Scotland, or England in search of new opportunities. Many immigrants were young, strong men, but just as often, young families with women and children made the trip. Even though the famine had not yet peaked in the early 1830s, life was challenging, and the promise of a new start was enticing. These immigrants were driven by the hope of finding greater economic opportunities, better living conditions, and the chance to build a more prosperous future.

The journey from Europe itself was fraught with hardship. Immigrants faced overcrowded and often unsanitary conditions on ships, leading to outbreaks of disease. Many endured weeks of rough seas, inadequate food, and limited fresh water. Upon arrival, the challenges continued. They had to navigate a new and unfamiliar environment, often with little money and no immediate employment. The hope of new opportunities was shadowed by the harsh reality that some people left and were never heard from again, disappearing into the New World, perhaps meeting an untimely end.

Canadian cities such as Halifax, Nova Scotia, and Saint John, New Brunswick, served as ports of entry for many of these Irish immigrants. An estimated sixty thousand Irish immigrants came to Canada between 1831 and 1850. Most of the people immigrating to North America at this time, before the famine, were Protestants. The timber industry in these cities called to the young men, offering employment and the potential for a stable income. These cities also often represented just the first step in their New World experience. As sea routes and land routes became more accessible, many immigrants who initially arrived in Canada eventually made their way to American cities. Some traveled to the port in Saint John to catch the new "ferry" service to Portland and then on to destinations farther south. Advertisements in newspapers provided these immigrants with information on how to reach America, further facilitating their journey to new opportunities.

Once in Canada or the United States, immigrants faced hardships. They encountered discrimination and prejudice, often being viewed as outsiders or threats to the local job market. Housing was typically cramped and inadequate, with entire families squeezed into small, poorly ventilated rooms. Employment opportunities, while more plentiful than in Ireland, were often limited to low-paying, labor-intensive jobs.

Despite these challenges, the resilience and determination of these immigrants helped them persevere. They formed tightknit communities, supporting each other through the difficulties of settlement. Their contributions to the development of Canada and the United States were significant, laying the foundations for future generations. The story of these pre-famine immigrants is a testament to the enduring human spirit, their legacy woven into the very fabric of North American history. They came with dreams of a better life, driven by hope, and faced numerous obstacles, yet their journey and sacrifices helped shape the nations they would come to call home.

Many of the passengers on board the *Royal Tar* were moving from New Brunswick to Portland, where the winters were milder. The camaraderie on the boat was significant, with some passengers even cooking meals together in their quarters in the steerage section.

The *Royal Tar* specifically targeted immigrants in Saint John with advertisements in the local paper. Stops were made in Eastport and Portland. New Brunswick Courier, *1836.*

We know the survivor stories because they survived; those who died never had their stories told. The people who died that day on the *Royal Tar* may have ceased to exist in the historical record. Some were traveling from Ireland via Canada to Boston, perhaps in search of a new life, an adventure, or escape from a bad situation elsewhere. Every journey by car, foot, boat, or plane is an opportunity for something new, but it is fraught with danger. Sometimes, we don't make it to our destination, and life changes forever. For the thirty-three people who lost their lives on the *Royal Tar* that day, their journeys ended tragically.

Biographical Information About Passengers

In 1832, the General Assembly of New Brunswick enacted a statute entitled "An Act to Regulate Vessels Arriving from the United Kingdom with Passengers and Emigrants." Passengers disembarking in New Brunswick ports were required to pay five shillings, and their names were added to a list. These lists still exist today and have been archived by the Provincial Archives of New Brunswick.

A comparison of these lists of emigrants who arrived at Saint John with the passenger list from the *Royal Tar* led to the identification of six individuals appearing on both lists. This provided valuable insights into their backgrounds and lives before boarding the *Royal Tar*. These are their stories.

- In 1834, the passenger ship *Robert Burns* sailed from Londonderry, Ireland, to Saint John. Aboard the ship was a young woman, Margarite Cochran, age twenty. She left her hometown of Enniskillen in Northern Ireland. In the official passenger lists, her occupation was listed as "Spinster." Perhaps she spent two years with relatives in or around Saint John and then in 1836 decided to take a chance again and head to America. Records indicate that a Peggy Cochran died on the *Royal Tar*.
- Thomas Mahoney sailed from Kinsale, Ireland, aboard the *Independence* and arrived in Saint John in 1834. An experienced seaman, it is likely that when he arrived in New Brunswick, he would have sought work on other ships. While he was a passenger on the *Royal Tar*, it could be that he was headed to Portland or eventually Boston, looking for more work after joining family in one of those American cities.
- Dennis O'Brien, a laborer from Ireland, sailed from Dublin on the *Breeze* in 1834 when he was twenty. He probably had no trouble finding work in Saint John, with all the building taking place in the city and shipyards in the area. But as is often

the case with young men, he may have sought the adventure of a new place, a new market for his skills. He bought his ticket to Portland and boarded the *Royal Tar* in October 1836.

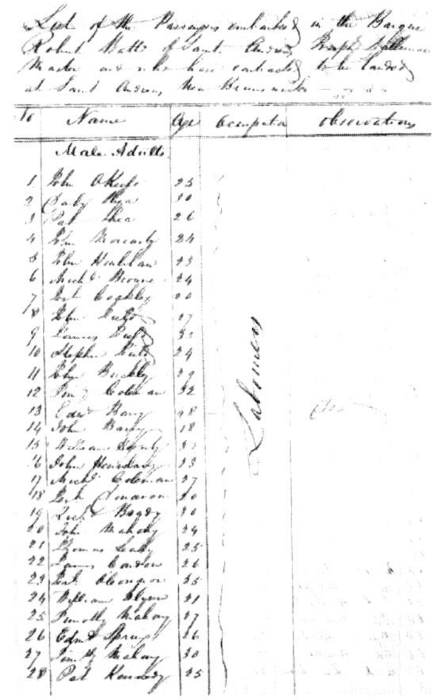

Handwritten records of all immigrants arriving in Saint John were made, indicating their name, city of origin, the ship they arrived on, age, and occupation. These records are accessible online today. *Provincial Archives of New Brunswick.*

- Another Irishman, John Hogan, came to Saint John at the age of twenty-six in 1833. He sailed on the *Ewerretta* from the port in Londonderry. He was also employed as a laborer but may have felt as if he had gone as far as he could in New Brunswick. It is possible that he married a young woman named Mary, and perhaps together they decided to take their chances and head to Boston. They purchased tickets on the *Royal Tar* for the October 21 voyage and may have been thrilled to be traveling on board with exotic animals from far and wide.
- In 1836, Owen Doherty was twenty-six years old. He had arrived in Saint John three years prior. A laborer from Malin, Ireland, he came to Canada aboard the *Trial*, perhaps looking for a better life for himself. He was on board the *Royal Tar* on that fateful journey and was one of the lucky ones. Owen lived and most likely continued on to Portland, Boston, or beyond with a tale of survival to tell.
- Patrick Moore was aboard the *Sea Horse* in 1833 when it came to Saint John. He was an eighteen-year-old from County Kildare in Ireland whose occupation on the passenger list was given as "gentleman." Little is known about how he spent his time in the years after landing in Saint John, but he was aboard the *Royal Tar* in October 1836, one of many passengers traveling with the menagerie on that fateful trip. Patrick survived the sinking and made it to his ultimate destination.

People Aboard the *Royal Tar*

On October 21, 1836, ninety-three people boarded the *Royal Tar* at Peter's Wharf in Saint John, New Brunswick. While the stories of all these individuals are not fully known, research and old newspaper archives have revealed the backstories of some. The official manifest, maintained by the captain, indicated that there were a total of seventy-two passengers and twenty-one crew members. However, this figure is just an estimate, and the actual number was likely higher. It was not uncommon for small children and infants traveling with their parents to be omitted. Some say there were six to eight children onboard who were not part of the official list.

- Captain Thomas Reed was the first, and only, commander of the *Royal Tar*. A native of Saint John, Captain Reed was forty-six at the time he took command of the newly commissioned *Royal Tar*. He was married to Frances Reed, and together they had six children. His new route aboard the *Royal Tar* split his time away from home. The boat left Saint John on Wednesdays and returned from the trip to Portland on Monday.
- Other crew members included: Francis Black, mate; N. Marshal, engineer; J. Kehoe, second engineer; W.G. Brown, steward; and Margaret Watts (sometimes referred to as Margaret Burr), stewardess.
- W.H. Harrison was twenty-four years old and had spent the summer working on the bridge being built over the Saint John River near Saint John, New Brunswick. The work was hard, and by the time fall came, he was ready for a break. He was determined to take a break and visit friends in Upper Canada (which today is part of Ontario). At the time, the best way for a traveler from New Brunswick to get to Upper Canada was to take a steamer to Portland, Maine, and continue from there. Harrison bought a ticket on the *Royal Tar*.
- J.T. Sherwood was aboard the *Royal Tar* in October 1836. He was on his way to Portland to serve as British consul there. Sherwood, a seasoned traveler, was aboard the steam brig *New York* when it sank in the waters off Maine in 1822 or 1823. He didn't let that experience stop him, however, and was eager to board the *Royal Tar*, described by her owners as the "safest ship on the sea."

- Henry H. Fuller oversaw the traveling menagerie. After touring Nova Scotia and New Brunswick for most of the summer and fall, he and his workers were eager to get back to Boston before the weather got too cold. They had attempted to book passage earlier in the month on a ship from Yarmouth, Nova Scotia, but were unable to find a suitable vessel for their group. Moving quicker than their usual pace, the menagerie made the trip from Yarmouth to Saint John in two to three weeks and looked forward to a relatively quick trip down the coast. The summer had been fruitful, but the schedule was bruising, and all were looking forward to a rest.

CHAPTER 3

THE TRAVELING CIRCUS

The circus we know today, with its big top, side shows, and three rings of daring acts, is quite different from what existed in the early 1800s. According to Stuart Thayer's book *American Circus Anthology: Essays of the Early Years*, the earliest displays of wild animals in America began in rural taverns. Hunters would bring bears, deer, mountain lions, or other wild animals they had captured to these taverns to display, likely while boasting of their own cunning tracking skills. Emblematic of such exhibitions was the dancing bear, perhaps on a leash and maybe wearing a jaunty top hat.

This form of entertainment soon expanded to include exotic animals, as sailors brought monkeys, parrots, and other smaller creatures to ports when they returned from their adventures. These animals were often their pets, but for the most part, they had not been seen by the American public. Larger animals from faraway lands were often captured and brought to our shores as babies. With the addition of these mysterious creatures, a new spectacle emerged. People were willing to pay to see these wild animals. Whether they were caged, secured to a stake by a rope or chain, riding on their owner's shoulders, or performing simple tricks, these animals could draw in crowds and their money.

The introduction of exotic animals had a profound impact on the entertainment industry. These creatures fascinated audiences and boosted the popularity of traveling shows. The novelty of seeing such animals up close created a sense of wonder and excitement, leading to increased attendance and revenue for exhibitors. This, in turn, spurred the growth of the circus industry, as more entrepreneurs recognized the lucrative potential of featuring exotic animals in their shows.

The inclusion of larger animals into the mix precipitated the need for handlers and showmen. These individuals had a range of responsibilities. They oversaw the health, safety, and welfare of the animals, ensuring they were properly fed, watered, and sheltered. Handlers also trained the animals to perform tricks and routines, employing techniques that required patience and skill. Additionally, they were responsible for transporting the animals safely between locations, a task that involved meticulous planning and logistical coordination.

By their very nature, these animal shows had to be mobile. People usually didn't pay to see the same animals do the same tricks more than once or twice. The shows had to move to new markets. Front men, sometimes called exhibitors, traveled to villages, arranging to set up their exhibits at taverns, stables, or town squares along the East Coast of the United States. They charged an entrance fee, usually a quarter for adults or fifteen cents for children under the age of ten. The group would stay in an area until the crowds diminished and it seemed that everyone who was going to come had already seen the animals. Then they would pack up and move to the next village.

These traveling circuses, also known as menageries, were initially small, but they brought animals from around the world to small villages and large cities across the United States and Canada. Elephants were one of the most significant draws for the traveling circus. Standing, on average, over twelve feet tall and weighing more than five tons, these giants held a special place in the imagination for many. When the gentle ways and intelligence of these animals were added to the allure, the prized elephant became a fixture in the traveling circus.

It all began in 1796, when the first elephant arrived in New York, marking the start of America's fixation with the circus. This elephant toured up and down the East Coast, drawing crowds from all over who were willing to pay a quarter to see this massive creature. The elephant may have performed a few tricks or displayed its great strength, but people were also paying for a look at this rare, unusual, and massive animal. Then, in 1812, an elephant was presented at a circus performance, and that's when the magic truly happened. The elephant became synonymous with "circus."

Old Bet

No discussion about circus elephants would be complete without mentioning Old Bet, an African elephant bought at auction for a mere twenty dollars. The first known reference to Old Bet dates back to 1804, when she was already the star attraction in a Boston-based menagerie. Four years later, she was purchased by Hachaliah Bailey, the founder of the Bailey Circus, which would eventually merge into the world-renowned Barnum and Bailey Circus. As the star of these traveling shows, Old Bet was paraded from town to town, too large to be caged, with her handlers always close by. This created a unique problem for the menagerie: as Old Bet walked down local roads, curious onlookers could easily catch a glimpse of her without paying the admission fee, which significantly cut into the circus's profits.

To combat this loss of revenue, the circus adopted the practice of traveling at night, ostensibly to keep their own horses and local animals calm, but likely more so to avoid being seen by the locals free of charge. However, the resourceful townsfolk quickly devised a way to thwart this tactic. They began setting up large haystacks along the routes Old Bet traveled and positioning lookouts ready to signal when the menagerie was near. As soon as the alert was given and Old Bet approached, the haystacks were set ablaze, lighting up the night and offering everyone a free, fiery spectacle of the great elephant.

Not to be outdone, the menagerie struck back with a clever ruse of their own. They sent horsemen ahead of Old Bet, shouting, "Mile up! Mile up!" to deceive the locals into thinking the elephant was about to pass by. The haystacks would be ignited prematurely, and by the time Old Bet actually arrived, the fires had dwindled to mere smoldering embers, leaving the onlookers with little more than a hint of smoke and a glimpse of darkness.

The tension between the circus and the locals was palpable, driven by a clash of interests—one seeking to profit from the marvel of Old Bet and the other determined to witness the spectacle without paying a dime. This ongoing cat-and-mouse game reflected the broader conflict between the traveling circus and the rural communities it passed through, where cultural and economic differences often sparked resentment and creative resistance.

Old Bet's story took a tragic turn in July 1816 when a local man, driven by a mix of moral indignation and resentment, shot her in the head as she and her circus were en route to Boston and Maine. He later justified his actions by claiming it was criminal for people to pay twenty-five cents to see a "worthless" animal and that they shouldn't be traveling on a Sunday anyway. Despite the severity of his crime, the man faced only a brief three-day stint in jail, a meager punishment for the loss of the circus's beloved star and a stark reminder of the tensions that simmered beneath the surface in these early encounters between rural America and the world of spectacle and entertainment.

Other Animals

Elephants and their handlers may have been the stars of these shows, but traveling menageries often included a variety of animals. Hunters and poachers traveled far and wide, to Asia and Africa, South America and Australia, to capture exotic animals. Lions, camels, primates, and exotic snakes were on the list of animals purchased by various traveling menageries across the United States. Also on that list of animals were things like "Unicorn" and "Papio." The unicorn was, of course, a rhinoceros, and the Papio was most likely a baboon. Misidentification of animals was frequent, but no one really seemed to be concerned about that. A menagerie in 1815 claimed to have a cougar in its collection of animals that was the "largest of the tiger kind ever brought to this country. It was three feet tall and eight feet long." It is suspected now that they had a jaguar.

Animals were advertised in one town or city and then did not appear with the menagerie in the next. Replacements, substitutions, and confusion marked the reporting of the animals on display. But despite this, paying patrons were still treated to a view of animals the likes of which they had never seen before.

Procuring the animals from the plains of Africa or jungles of southeast Asia was a perilous and often deadly business. Hunting parties of fifty or more men, usually on horseback and traveling with dogs, entered these remote areas tasked with bringing back "specimens" for these traveling circuses. Charles Ellms described one such hunting expedition in his book *The Tragedy of the Seas; or Sorrow on the Ocean, Lake, and River, from Shipwreck, Plague, Fire, and Famine*. It follows one hunting party that set out from the Cape of Good Hope and moved north into South Africa. This team of men, dogs, and horses walked 2,300 miles over seven weeks in search of wild animals. They were hunters, after the prize of an animal pelt or meat. But they were also looking for young animals or babies to sell to traveling circuses or zoos in Europe or America. After seven weeks of travel, they found themselves pursuing a lion known to be in the area. It had recently killed a domesticated gazelle owned by a local guide. The book continues to describe the confrontation with the lion in gory detail.

The local guides cornered the lion among rocks in the rugged terrain of the savannah. The lead hunters could see the "glaring eye-balls of his lionship" peering out from his hiding spot. Without waiting for the rest of the hunting party, the lead hunter shot at the lion, sure of his ability to take it down. He either missed or just irritated the lion because the beast attacked. In an instant, the lion, estimated to be seven feet in length, jumped on one of the guides, tearing the flesh and breaking bones of one of his arms. At the sound of the shots, the rest of the hunting party ran to the scene, where the lion was described as "standing over [the man] in an attitude of exultation." Initially hesitant to take a shot, for fear that they would accidentally hit their comrade, but also afraid that they were about to see him devoured by the lion, the group decided to work as one and shoot at the lion's head on a given signal. They were successful, and the mighty lion fell, dead, on the unfortunate and injured hunter, who, according to Ellms's description, "expected every moment to be his last." The group was soon doubly pleased with their kill. The animal they had killed was actually a lioness, and "and on entering her den, they were rejoiced to find a pair of beautiful cubs, which were now conveyed away without molestation." These two lion cubs were later sold to Macomber, Welch & Company Menagerie.

Life with a Traveling Circus

Life in a traveling menagerie was tough—long hours, hard work, and constant danger. The circus workers lived a nomadic life, moving from town to town across the United States and Canada, creating a sense of community and sometimes even family among them. Animal handlers and trainers were especially valued and often stayed with the circus longer than other workers.

The introduction of canvas tents around 1825 revolutionized the traveling circus, transforming it into a truly mobile spectacle. Circus proprietor J. Purdy Brown was among the first to take a circus on the road using a large canvas tent, debuting this innovation in a field near Brewster, New York, belonging to William Storm. The appearance of the tent alone created a stir—people flocked to see this enormous structure, not for the promise of a performance but simply to marvel at the engineering feat. There was widespread speculation about how many yards of cloth had been used to create the tent, and its mere presence became an attraction. For several days, the tent stood as a curiosity, drawing crowds eager to admire it. Only after this initial excitement did the circus begin to perform, offering a new kind of entertainment experience that was no longer confined to permanent buildings or fairgrounds.

This canvas innovation allowed circuses to set up in a variety of locations—cornfields, town squares, and any open space that could accommodate the tent. Gone were the days of relying on costly and fire-prone permanent structures. The circus could now bring its exotic animals and thrilling acts directly to the people, reaching audiences in even the most remote areas. For the cost of admission, usually around a quarter, spectators could see elephants, camels, lions, and exotic snakes—creatures that most people had only ever heard of, let alone seen with their own eyes. The allure of these exotic animals was powerful, and many were more than willing to pay for the opportunity to witness such wonders. The portability of the tent enabled the circus to expand its reach, making it a fixture in towns across the country and solidifying its place as a beloved form of entertainment in nineteenth-century America.

With tents and mobility came a need for more workers and wagons. The wagons not only provided transportation but also served as shelters for workers and animals at different sites. The animals, especially horses and sometimes elephants, did double duty, carrying wagons, people, and supplies from town to town. Skilled teamsters and handlers were essential for this operation.

Traveling menageries moved at a leisurely pace, averaging only about fifteen miles a day. This slow progress was dictated by the need to accommodate the animals, particularly large ones like elephants, and the necessity to carefully navigate the rough and often unpaved roads of the time. The journey from Boston to Portland, Maine, which spans roughly one hundred miles, would typically take about seven days. However, these seven days were not just about covering distance; they also presented valuable opportunities for the menagerie to set up temporary shows in small towns or farmers' fields along the route. Each stop allowed the circus to entertain the local populace, drawing in crowds eager to catch a glimpse of exotic animals and thrilling performances. These impromptu performances helped the menagerie supplement its income, making the most of every mile traveled and turning the journey itself into a series of profitable engagements. The slow pace of travel also allowed word of their arrival to spread ahead of them, creating hype and ensuring that crowds would be waiting at each new stop.

Menageries showcased human dominance over the wild world, displaying exotic animals like lions, tigers, elephants, and ostriches. The tamers or handlers would often put on demonstrations, eliciting awe and fear in the locals. These events likely sparked dreams and left lasting impressions on the audiences.

Menageries were unique in that everyone—animals and humans alike—played a vital role, seamlessly blending work with entertainment and mobility with spectacle. Take, for example, the horses in a traveling circus: they weren't just animals performing tricks; they were symbols of the intertwined nature of labor and entertainment in the circus world. Menageries, whether traveling solo or as part of a larger circus with acts and sideshows, lent an air of legitimacy and social acceptance to the circus, which was often viewed with skepticism by more conservative members of society.

The circus, with its colorful acts, daring performers, and occasional brush with the unsavory—like pickpockets and the perceived indecency of skimpy costumes—frequently drew criticism from Protestant church members and other moral authorities. In contrast, the educational value of the menagerie, which showcased exotic animals and provided a form of natural history education, was more palatable to these communities. Circus owners quickly recognized this difference in perception and became adept at tailoring their presentations to suit their audiences. In towns where the circus was met with suspicion or outright hostility, they would downplay the more sensational aspects and emphasize the educational merits of the menagerie, presenting it as a form of educational exhibition rather than mere entertainment.

This strategic interchangeability of the terms *menagerie* and *circus* allowed circus owners to navigate the cultural and moral landscape of nineteenth-century America with finesse. By promoting the menagerie as an educational experience, they could gain entry into communities that might otherwise have shunned the circus. In more permissive or entertainment-hungry towns, the full spectacle of the circus—with its daring acts—would be on display. This flexibility not only broadened the circus's appeal but also helped it flourish in a society where the lines between education and entertainment, respectability and spectacle, were often blurred. The menagerie, with its promise of education and exposure to the wonders of the natural world, became the key to unlocking new markets and winning over skeptics, ensuring the circus's place in the fabric of American life.

Anticipation was the prime marketing approach of circuses and menageries in the early 1800s. There was much build-up in the weeks and days before a menagerie arrived in town. A town was plastered with advertisements and posters in the weeks leading up to the performances. The anticipation grew and grew. The spectacle of the wagons, with their ornate decorations and glimpses of exotic animals, drew crowds when the circus rolled into town. Other acts may have journeyed with a traveling menagerie for a time, dropping in and out over the course of a season. Brass bands, displays of exotic serpents and birds, or even wax museums were often part of the show. The traveling menagerie was somewhat of a fluid entity with the animals as the main event but occasionally with other sideshows in tow as well.

The Zoological Institute

The early 1830s were prosperous times in the United States, benefiting everyone, including those in the entertainment business. This period, between the Panic of 1819 and the Panic of 1837, saw people with expendable income willing to spend fifteen to twenty-five cents to see exotic animals. Many entrepreneurs and investors followed the example set by Hachaliah Bailey and began to acquire and tour with their own set of exotic animals. This led to competition and overlap, with differing menageries vying for the same hard-earned quarters of the general public. There was a call for some type of organization. A loose confederation of around twelve menageries and three circuses decided to join forces. This partnership would allow for resource sharing and collaborative efforts A group of the menageries' owners met on January 14, 1835, at the Elephant Hotel in Somers, New York. There, they signed the Articles of Association of the Zoological Institute. The document still exists, although much of the ink has faded, rendering the document largely unreadable today.

Tracking the lineage of different traveling menageries in the northeastern part of the United States has proven to be difficult due to sparse records from the early 1830s. Names and owners often changed, but the variety of animals ensured a constant stream of eager customers. The purpose of the Zoological Institute was to "move generally diffuse and promote the knowledge of a natural history and gratify rational curiosity." In all, 135 signatures graced the document. This included nearly all the menagerie owners of the Northeast and businessmen who relied on the shows for income, including printers who made posters and advertisements for the groups. One of the charters of the group was to set routes and schedules, creating a loose monopoly of the traveling circus business in the East.

A poster advertising the Zoological Institute of New York. The Institute #10 of Boston would have had similar advertisements. *Jared W. Bell,* The Association's Celebrated and Extensive Menagerie and Aviary from the Zoological Institute in the City of New-York, 1835. *Woodcut, engraving, and letterpress print on paper, 114 x77 314 in. Collection of Shelburne Museum, gift of Harry T. Peters, Jr., Natalie Peters, and Natalie Webster. 1959–67.78. Photography by Andy Duback.*

This confederation lasted about two years. There was another national economic panic in 1837, brought on by changes to the banking system, a failure in wheat crops nationwide, and international economic downturns. This turn of events stressed the resources of the average citizen, eliminating their expendable incomes for frivolous entertainment. Although the Zoological Institute disbanded a short two years after it was formed, many of the ideas and practices set out by its charter endured.

UNIT #10 FROM THE ZOOLOGICAL INSTITUTE OF BOSTON

One such menagerie, Unit #10 from the Zoological Institute of Boston, toured from Boston into Nova Scotia and New Brunswick in the summer of 1836. Newspaper archives and other sources have attributed other names to this specific menagerie, including Macomber, Welch & Company Menagerie and Fuller's Menagerie (or Fuller's Caravan). Henry H. Fuller oversaw Unit #10 in the summer of 1836, so it is no surprise that his name is associated with the group in many of the historical resources.

As was usual, the menagerie was not alone. Again, the research has proven to be vague and contradictory at times, but the majority of sources agreed that the menagerie was not alone that summer. Traveling with it was Burgess's collection of serpents and birds, Dexter's Locomotive Museum, a brass band, and perhaps a waxworks museum. There were at least six horses to not only perform but also pull the wagons. The menagerie was traveling with an elephant, two dromedaries, two lionesses, one royal Bengal tiger, a gnu, and a pair of pelicans. Exotic snakes traveled with Burgess's company and the locomotive museum, which was not related to trains, as we might think today, but was simply a traveling museum of various oddities.

For twenty-five cents, people could enter into a world unlike anything they had ever seen. Animals from around the world were there for all who were willing to pay to see them. The star of the show was Mogul, an Asian elephant. According to the elephant database maintained by Dan Koehl of Sweden, Mogul was a male elephant that arrived in Boston aboard the ship in the company of a rhinoceros. After arriving in Boston, Mogul was exhibited at Lion Tavern in Boston in 1832. He was bought and sold several times before eventually landing with Macomber, Welch & Company, with whom he toured in the spring and summer of 1836.

Mogul was loved by all who encountered him. Understanding of the intelligence of an elephant in the 1830s was limited, but Mogul's handlers grew to recognize how intelligent, stubborn, and expressive this giant animal could be. One story, from the *Newburyport Herald* on February 24, 1835, explained how Mogul could become impatient and demanding of his food. In one report, his handler had other business to attend to, and a substitute caregiver oversaw Mogul. When his handler returned for the night, he assumed that all was well and Mogul had been fed. The man crawled into bed and had barely laid his head on his pillow before:

> *His Mightiness Mogul who had stepped over the bar, three and a half feet high, came growling along to his bedside. The keeper started up, and the elephant at once twisted his trunk around one of his arms, and led him directly beneath the stairs, where, by oversetting an empty barrel, he not only intimated to his master that he was supperless but that he had no prospect of any food from the usual source. Nor would he suffer the keeper again to retire till he had ascended to the loft, and procured him the usual quantity of oats and potatoes.*

Traveling with an elephant like Mogul was always an adventure. Usually, while traveling from town to town, Mogul was flanked by two of his keepers, each on horseback. On one occasion, something startled him. It could have been a distant gunshot, an aggressive farm dog, or who knows what. He got so spooked that he took off in a sprint, leaving his keepers and their horses in the dust. He ran nearly six miles in just thirty minutes and then slowed to a jog as if nothing had happened.

Mogul had a weakness for the crisp New England apples that grew in the fall. He soon learned that by removing the upper rails of the fences that bounded apple orchards, he could get at the apples with little problem. When he had his fill, he would return to the road and rejoin the group, without needing instructions from his handlers.

Your entrance fee, perhaps dropped into a hat at the entrance to the tent, not only gave you a glimpse of the two lions captured following the death of their mother in South Africa but also got you an up-close look at the regal and noble "royal tiger of Bengal," which weighed nearly five hundred pounds and was said to be larger than any other tiger on exhibit in North America at the time. He was described as a truly gentle giant.

The tiger's early days were marked by violence and captivity. For three and a half relentless days, hunters scoured the wilderness, looking for a female tiger known to be in the area. The final confrontation was brutal: they clashed with the mother tiger, leaving her gravely wounded. Defeated, she crawled back to her underground den, leaving behind her young male cub. It was then, in the aftermath of that fierce battle, that the hunters seized the helpless cub, which was now destined to become a caged spectacle in the circus.

The young tiger cub grew up with his keepers, who were kind and provided the care and training needed to be an animal in a traveling menagerie. He grew up being touched and caressed by his handlers and would allow that to happen, even as he grew to his immense size. At one point, he became fascinated by a dog that traveled with the menagerie, barking at strangers and eating scraps. He would watch the dog's every move from his cage and seemed so interested in him that the handlers let the dog into the tiger's quarters. The dog and the tiger became fast friends, and "the tiger was not infrequently seen to fondle and lick the dog, and to regard him with even more tenderness than this animal usually does his mate." Sadly, the dog became ill a few weeks after this and died. This devastated the lonely tiger, which "moaned out his requiem, walking restlessly up and down the cage."

This menagerie also included a gnu, which was one of the "first specimens of this wonderfully constructed animal that had been introduced in this country." Macomber, Welch & Company sent a hunting party to Africa, with specific instructions to come back with a "horned horse" and to do whatever it took to procure one. The brutal events of this trip reflect the prevailing nineteenth-century belief that men had an inherent right to hunt animals for profit, highlighting the often-callous attitude of that era toward wildlife and nature.

Two hunting parties set out, searching for nearly two months before finally finding a large herd of gnu. One of the parties finally caught, after another month, three "furious animals," which they found nearly impossible to control. These wild animals could only be managed by "fettering their legs, and confining their heads by strong cords to their forelegs." It was tied as such that the animals began their trip from their home to faraway lands. The other party was searching an area that was experiencing a severe drought, and "their sufferings were for several days almost incredible, from the impossibility of obtaining food for their horses and themselves." They did manage to capture one lone gnu, after a long five months during which three of their party died. The capture of animals from Africa and Asia was a perilous undertaking, endangering human lives and altering the fate of the majestic animals they sought.

With these animals, and others in tow, Fuller's Menagerie set out from Boston in the early summer of 1836. At this time, the menagerie also included "rare curiosities," including "the anaconda, a live serpent from the island of Ceylon [currently Sri Lanka], two golden pheasants, the only ones in America, and several specimens of Talking Parrots."

After making its way through the Canadian Maritimes, the menagerie was exhibiting in Yarmouth, Nova Scotia, on Wednesday, September 28, 1863. The advertisement obtained from the *Yarmouth Herald* promised the following: "A very large elephant, with a splendid Eastern Saddle...will be exhibited under a spacious pavilion in Yarmouth, on Wednesday, Sept 28 and a few succeeding days, from 1 to 4 o'clock each day."

There were acts, but the idea was for the public to pay to see the animals in their cages.

The advertisement went on to indicate that the "keeper enters the Lion's cage at 3 pm. Animals fed at half past 3 PM The exercise of the highly trained Elephant Mogul—the feed of the wild beasts—the enter the Lion's Cage; and the performance in the Ring by the Monkey and Pony—form a truly astonishing and interesting exhibition." It should be noted that other accounts, specifically of the tragedy that follows, did not include monkeys in the list of animals. Other references to monkeys were made but not in the account of the fire and sinking.

In Yarmouth, the advertisement continued, suggesting that interested people should check out the posters exhibited at larger hotels in the area. The menagerie was in the Yarmouth area from September 5 to 27.

The following advertisement was placed in the *Yarmouth Herald* on August 19, 1836. From our seat today in history, we know that a suitable vessel was not found, and Fuller's Menagerie had about a month to make its way to Saint John, New Brunswick.

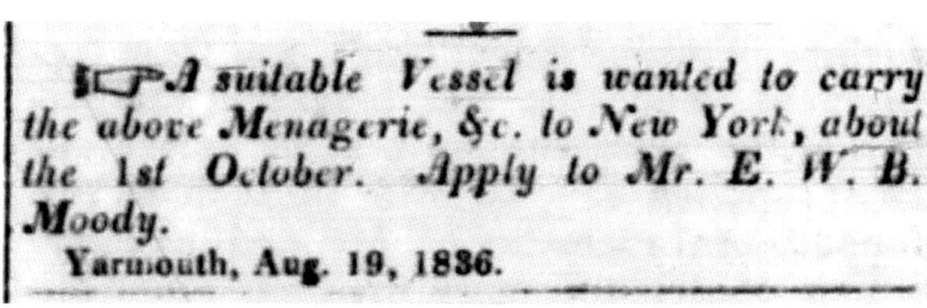

☞*A suitable Vessel is wanted to carry the above Menagerie, &c. to New York, about the 1st October. Apply to Mr. E. W. B. Moody.*

Yarmouth, Aug. 19, 1836.

Fuller's Menagerie placed an ad looking for a ship to carry the entire circus to New York. They ended up making alternative plans. Yarmouth Herald, *August 19, 1836.*

Circus hands were given room and board, but their actual salary was presented at the end of the season. Their pay was tied to the success of the circus and the crowds it drew in. That October, when the menagerie arrived at the docks in Saint John to head back to Portland and points beyond, the hands received their summer wages.

CHAPTER 4

THE NORMAL, USUAL TRIP

On Monday, October 17, 1836, the *Royal Tar* returned to Saint John from its weekly trip to Portland. According to the schedule, the next trip was set to leave from Peter's Wharf on Friday. Captain Thomas Reed and his crew likely visited their families, checking in on their loved ones. There were also some unusual preparations for the Friday, October 21 trip. Reed learned upon arriving back at port that they would be carrying a traveling circus on the next trip. This circus included caged animals in special wagons, as well as an elephant. The elephant, along with at least six horses and two camels, would be chained on deck, while the cages with lions and a tiger would go below deck. Cages of exotic snakes, birds, and a gnu completed the unique passenger list. Concerned about space, the decision was made to remove two of the lifeboats to accommodate the unusual passengers, leaving only two lifeboats on board, one larger than the other. Some were concerned that the deck might not support the added weight of an elephant, so carpenters added extra bracing to the ceiling near the boiler, below the spot where the great elephant would be chained.

While those preparations continued, Fuller's Menagerie rolled into Saint John. And what a wonder it must have been. Horses, adorned with bright bridles, pulled wagons carrying the cages of two lionesses and a majestic Bengal tiger. Other horses pulled the show wagon, or omnibus. Mogul, the elephant, walked steadily along with his trainers at his side. The menagerie was accompanied by an exhibit of waxworks and a brass band.

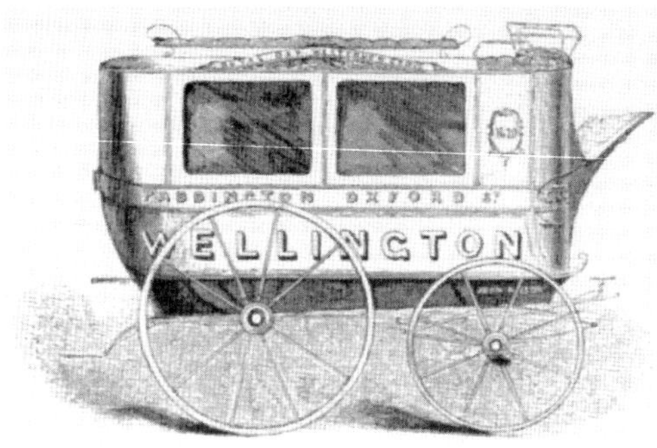

This omnibus is similar to the one pulled from town to town by the horses in Fuller's Menagerie. It may have carried the lions or the tiger for all to see. *Henry Charles Moore, public domain, via Wikimedia Commons.*

A FINAL PERFORMANCE

People from Saint John and the surrounding areas came to the corner of Charlotte and Union Streets that Thursday evening to watch the final performance of the circus that season. They were undoubtedly wowed by the tricks and feats performed by the animals. Mogul likely charmed the crowd as children watched with mouths agape, especially during the feeding of the lions and the tiger.

The circus performers, though weary from their summer tour, seemed to find a renewed energy for this final show. The anticipation of returning home soon likely spurred them on, and the sight of the eager faces in the crowd gave them a final burst of enthusiasm. The air was filled with the sound of excited chatter. As the brass band struck up a lively tune, the performers took their places.

The horses, with their bright bridles gleaming under the lanterns, trotted out in perfect unison, pulling the ornate wagons. The crowd gasped as the cages with the lionesses and the Bengal tiger came into view. The majestic tiger, with its striking stripes, paced back and forth, occasionally pausing to stare at the audience with piercing, curious eyes. Perhaps he was scanning the crowd, looking for his canine friend from years ago.

Mogul was the star of the show. His trainers led him into the ring, where he performed a series of tricks that left the audience in awe. He lifted heavy logs with ease, balanced on a small platform, and even used his trunk to paint a picture, much to the delight of the children. The highlight of the evening was the feeding of the lions and the tiger. As the trainers carefully approached the cages with slabs of raw meat, the crowd fell silent, their eyes wide with a mix of fear and fascination. The powerful roars of the feeding cats echoed through the night, adding an element of danger to the spectacle.

Today, a park stands at the corners of Charlotte and Union Streets in Saint John. This is approximately the site of the final performance of Fuller's Menagerie in October 1836. *Author's collection.*

Despite their exhaustion, the performers' passion for their craft shone through. The waxworks exhibit fascinated those who preferred a quieter form of entertainment, and the brass band played energetically, the music providing the perfect backdrop for the night's festivities.

After the performance, Fuller gathered his workers together for one last meeting of the season. This final payday was a highly anticipated event, and there was an air of excitement and relief as Fuller distributed the summer wages. The workers, pockets now heavy with specie, likely felt a mixture of pride and exhaustion as they reflected on the long, arduous months behind them.

The evening was filled with a celebratory spirit. Many of the workers might have ventured out into the lively streets of Saint John, seeking out local pubs to unwind and celebrate the end of a successful season. Laughter and cheers would have filled the air as they recounted their favorite moments and shared stories of their adventures on the road. The camaraderie among the circus workers, forged through countless performances and travels, was palpable.

However, the celebration was likely tempered with thoughts of the journey home. By the morning of October 21, the reality of their departure had set in. Most hands boarded the *Royal Tar*, their pockets jingling with the hard-earned wages they were eager to bring home to their families. There was a sense of anticipation and perhaps a touch of sadness as they prepared to leave behind the excitement of the circus for the comforts of home. The promise of seeing loved ones again kept their spirits high, despite the looming uncertainties of the voyage ahead.

A FESTIVE SENDOFF

Saint John is a hilly coastal town. The town's steep hills must have been a challenge for the horses and wagons as they crisscrossed the city early that Friday morning, making their way to Peter's Wharf. Mogul, however, reportedly mastered the technique of descending hills like a pro. His technique was described in the March 27, 1835 edition of *American Traveler*: "The pressure of his weight in these cases is so great that he uniformly resists the attraction of gravity as much as possible by bracing his forelegs and moving very slowly and cautiously, while he throws out his hind legs (letting himself down) and literally drags them after him down the hill."

The citizens of Saint John, who lined the streets and the area around Peter's Wharf, were treated not only to the brass band, the wagons, and glimpses of the circus animals but also to the spectacle of an elephant dragging his hind legs down the steep hills of their fine town.

The human passengers and crew boarded the *Royal Tar* as well on that cloudy morning. Captain Reed's manifest officially listed seventy-two passengers and twenty-one crew members. This may be inaccurate, as there

A view of Princess Street from near Peter's Wharf. These steep streets were navigated by Mogul and the circus wagons on their way to board the *Royal Tar*. *Author's collection.*

The view from Peter's Wharf (approximately), Saint John Harbor, New Brunswick. Partridge Island is visible in the distance. *Author's collection.*

were several infants and young children traveling with their parents who may not have been recorded. Spirits were high and festive as the brass band assembled on deck to play while the boat left Peter's Wharf.

Passenger W.H. Harrison noted, in an interview sixty years later, that when he boarded the *Royal Tar* on October 21, he knew he'd be traveling with Fuller's Menagerie: "I remember there were a number of horses, a large elephant, a number of wild animals and birds; also a large exhibit of waxwork."

Passengers lined the railings on deck as the boat pulled away from the wharf. Women waved handkerchiefs in the air, and children shouted and waved at everyone. Perhaps Mogul gave one last trumpeting cry as the *Royal Tar*, looking very much like Noah's Ark, steamed out toward Partridge Island.

Navigation in the 1830s

In the 1830s, navigation was an evolving art and science. Charts were becoming more accurate, thanks to increased exploration and improved mapping techniques. Mariners like Captain Reed of the *Royal Tar* relied heavily on these charts, as well as on sailing directions, known at the time as "routiers" or "rutters." These were essentially written instructions that detailed routes, landmarks, and compass directions, providing essential guidance for seafaring journeys.

An oft-traveled route, such as the one Captain Reed was taking, depended on recognizable landmarks and compass bearings. Mariners would use a variety of tools and techniques to determine their position and navigate the coastal waters. One such device was the impeller, a rotor or rotor blade that turned as water flowed past it. The rotations could be counted and translated into nautical miles, functioning much like an odometer for ships. This method was further refined with the use of the taffrail log, a type of mechanical log that utilized an impeller attached to a stiff line. As the impeller spun, it transmitted data to a dial mounted on the taffrail, providing real-time information on the distance traveled and current speed.

Coastal travel often relied on dead reckoning, a method of navigation that involved applying courses and distances made through the water from the last known observed position. The term "dead" in dead reckoning is believed to derive from "deduced" reckoning. This technique required a keen understanding of the vessel's speed, direction, and the time elapsed between known positions.

After the War of 1812, there was a significant increase in exploration, leading to a wealth of new information about weather, oceanography, and coastal geography. This era saw the sharing of knowledge among mariners and scholars, enhancing the accuracy of navigational charts and sailing directions. Early in the 1800s, commercial publishers produced many of these charts and sailing directions. However, by the mid-1800s, this task had increasingly become the responsibility of government agencies.

In 1807, Thomas Jefferson established the United States Coast Survey, tasked with mapping the U.S. coastlines. Although Captain Reed would have had access to some of these government-produced charts, he likely relied more heavily on dead reckoning and his intimate knowledge of coastal landmarks.

Mariners of the time often carried essential reference books like Nathaniel Bowditch's 1802 *The New American Practical Navigator* and *The American Coast Pilot*. These books provided directions along the East Coast, basic navigational techniques, and mathematical tables for common use. Bowditch's work, in particular, was a staple on many ships, offering comprehensive guidance that combined practical navigation tips with detailed mathematical formulas.

In the 1830s, weather prediction was still in its infancy. Mariners like Captain Reed had to rely on their observations of the sky, wind patterns, and barometric pressure changes. The appearance of mackerel clouds, for instance, was a known harbinger of approaching rain. The old adage "Red sky at night, sailor's delight. Red sky at morn, sailors be warned" has truth to it. A red sky at night indicates that the light rays from the sun are passing through a higher concentration of dust particles. This is indicative of high pressures and stable air from the west, a sign that good weather is coming. But when the skies are red in the morning, the rising sun's rays may be passing through air that has a lot of water vapor, and the good weather has passed by. This indicates that rain could be on the way. Captain Reed must have been worried when he awoke to a red sunrise before leaving Saint John. Sailors developed an intuitive understanding of weather patterns through experience and shared knowledge, which was crucial for making informed decisions during their voyages.

Despite the advancements in charts and navigational tools, the journey of the *Royal Tar* was deeply influenced by the superstitions of the sea, which held significant sway over the minds of sailors. According to maritime lore, the *Royal Tar* was doomed from the start. Superstitious sailors believed that whistling or playing wind instruments on board could summon storms, as the sounds were thought to mimic the wind and challenge it to blow harder. On the day of its departure, a brass band played as the ship left port, filling the air with music that some believed could provoke the wrath of the sea.

Additionally, the presence of women on board was considered an ill omen. It was a widely held belief that women distracted the crew and angered the gods of the sea, who would then send bad weather as a form of retribution. The *Royal Tar* was carrying not only many women but also several young girls, further heightening the sense of foreboding among the more superstitious sailors.

To make matters worse, the *Royal Tar* set sail on a Friday, a day considered especially unlucky by sailors. This superstition likely stemmed from its association with the crucifixion of Jesus Christ, and many believed that to begin a voyage on a Friday was to court disaster. As fate would have it, the *Royal Tar*, with its brass band playing and its many female passengers, departed from Saint John, New Brunswick, on Friday, October 21, 1836—a convergence of all the elements that, according to seafaring superstition, could only lead to catastrophe.

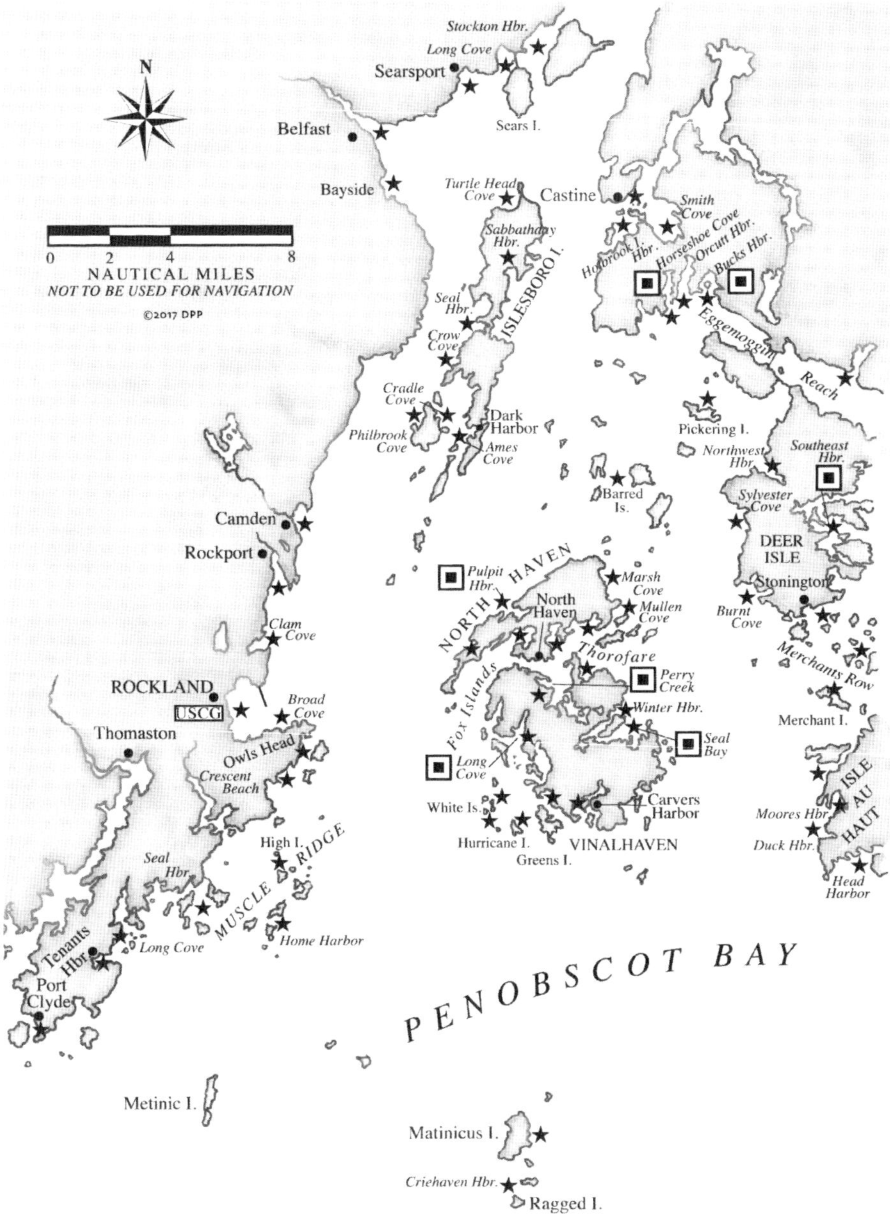

A current map of Penobscot Bay showing the islands and the mainland. The site of the wreck of the *Royal Tar* is to the northwest of Vinalhaven. *www.mainecoastguide.com.*

The Journey to Eastport

The short hop to Eastport was relatively smooth. But this was Friday afternoon. By evening, the winds had picked up, the seas had become choppy, and mackerel clouds foretold of rain to come within the next few days. Captain Reed, concerned about the conditions, called for the boat to be moved farther inland, into the Little River near Eastport, where they'd ride out the storm. They remained there for the next four days.

For four days, the *Royal Tar* sat in a sheltered spot along the Little River. Captain Reed watched the skies, reading his maps and consulting with his first mate about their chances of making it to Portland. The animals in their cages below deck became restless with the increased motion of the ship. Passengers got seasick from the smells of animals and cabbage soup and the choppy conditions. Supplies on board were insufficient for an extended trip; this was supposed to be a short trip to Portland. People, especially those in charge of the animals, grew concerned about their supplies of food and fresh water, but the rough conditions likely suppressed their appetites.

The circus animals, especially those below deck, required constant care and attention. Handlers ensured that the animals were fed and watered regularly, despite the challenging conditions. The sounds of restless lions and the pacing tiger added to the ship's already tense atmosphere. Special care was taken to keep Mogul calm. He was given extra rations of water and food, and his trainers stayed by his side, speaking to him in soothing tones to prevent any panic that might cause chaos on the crowded deck. The birds and smaller animals were covered with blankets to protect them from the cold and dampness, while the snake handlers kept a close watch on their charges to ensure they were secure and not stressed by the motion of the ship.

Resuming the Journey

Captain Reed tried again on Monday, October 24, to resume the trip. Away from shore, he and the crew found the seas heavy and a stiff wind still blowing from the northwest. Once again, the *Royal Tar* was moved closer to shore, this time into Machias Bay, where she was anchored until midnight. The trip was much slower than expected. By midnight, however, the winds were favorable, and they were on their way again.

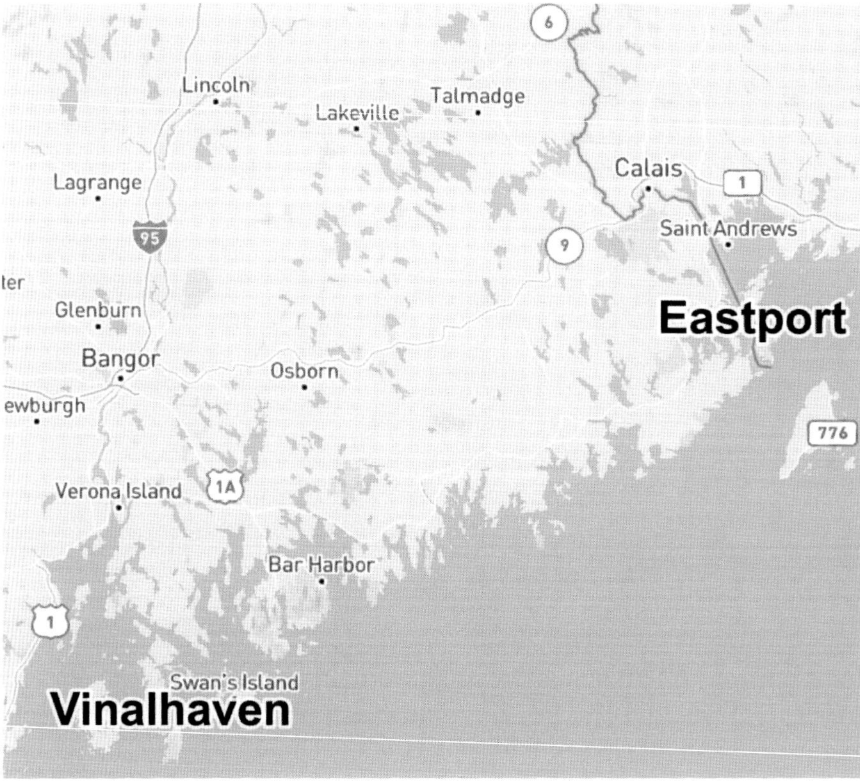

The *Royal Tar* left Eastport on Monday, October 24, and steamed to the point off Vinalhaven before catching fire and sinking on Tuesday, October 25. *Map by author using scribblemaps.com.*

Years later, Mrs. A.T. Small of Stonington, Maine, described watching the *Royal Tar* pass by her and her family shortly before it sank. In a letter to the editor of the *Argus* in 1912, she recalled seeing the circus ship as it traveled down the coast. She described how she and her two older siblings, accompanied by their father, rowed out in a small boat to see the larger, finer *Royal Tar*. Her recollections were vivid:

> *It was the first steamboat we had ever seen. As she came nearer, my father waved his hat, and the men on board did the same, and the women waved their handkerchiefs. There was one lady who came to the side of the boat. She was dressed in black with a white shawl over her shoulders and a handkerchief over her hair, which was white. She waved her hand, and as she did, I saw the jewels on her hand glistening in the bright sunshine. She said something in which the name of God was plainly heard.*

CHAPTER 5

A SHIP ENGULFED IN FLAMES

The trip was finally underway again, and the *Royal Tar* was making good progress. The winds had picked up, and the seas were choppy, but they were on track to reach Portland the next day. As the wind began to blow a "hearty gale" from the northwest, Captain Reed decided to turn the ship into the Fox Island Thoroughfare for shelter. Passengers milled around the deck, enjoying a breath of fresh air after being cooped up with the animals and each other for days. Many were heading to the dining room for the midday meal. Some handlers checked on Mogul and the caged animals below deck, while the firemen and engine men tended to the boiler. Captain Reed took a short break to speak with some passengers, leaving the second engineer, Mr. N. Marshall, in control of the ship.

At about 1:30 p.m. on October 25, the son of the pilot, Mr. Atkins, made a discovery that would alter the course of events. He was in the boiler room, possibly admiring the lions pacing restlessly in their cages or engrossed in a conversation with some of the younger firemen, who were spinning exaggerated tales of their daring exploits. As he moved past the massive, rumbling boiler, something unusual caught his eye. He had passed by that boiler numerous times already that day and countless times throughout the entire trip. Having spent years by his father's side, learning the intricacies of steamship operations, the young boy was intimately familiar with every nook and cranny of the boiler room. His keen eyes immediately recognized that something was amiss.

As he glanced at the boiler sight gauge, he did a double take. The lowest portion of the gauge was essentially empty. There was no water visible through the sight, indicating a serious problem with the boiler. The water level had been allowed to get too low, signaling imminent danger. Panicked, the boy ran to his father to report his discovery. His father, feeling a growing sense of dread, hurried to check the boiler himself. Confirming the boy's observation, he quickly alerted Marshall. However, Marshall, perhaps distracted or overworked, didn't take the warning seriously. With misplaced confidence, he asserted his expertise as the second engineer, dismissing the concern with, "Oh, don't worry about that. We've got water enough." With that, he went about his duties, unaware of the implications of his dismissal.

This proved to be a fatal mistake. As the passengers sat down to their afternoon meal, the crew below deck scrambled to address the issue. Not long after the initial discovery, around 2:00 p.m., the boiler grew red-hot. Without water to cool the parts, the steel became dangerously overheated. The firemen tried desperately to remedy the situation. Running into the pilothouse, the second engineer alerted Captain Reed, according to an article in the October 1965 issue of *Yankee Magazine*. The article includes a frantic conversation between the two men:

> *Captain Reed: "What's the matter, Marshall? Seasick?"*
> *Marshall: "No, Captain, it's worse than that. We've got to anchor and fill the boilers."*
> *Reed: "Well, we'll ease along until eight bells when we'll be close to Vinalhaven, and then we can water up."*
> *Marshall: "No! We can't wait that long. We've got to anchor now! The boilers are red hot, sir, red hot and smoking."*

According to the *Yankee Magazine* article, Captain Reed stared at Marshall for a moment, shocked at the news he was hearing. It seemed impossible that such an elementary mistake could have been made. But seeing in his assistant engineer's face that this was indeed the truth, Reed reportedly said, "Go back to the engine room, Marshall, and tend to your duties."

Moments later, Reed called for the anchor to be dropped. The fire in the furnace was extinguished, and the boat stopped moving, save for the up and down of the waves. The passengers must have felt the change and wondered what was happening. Those closest to the doors might have heard a vague commotion below. A curious young girl, around ten years old, leaving her parents' side, heard Mogul trumpet and the horses whinny. Perhaps she

A drawing of the *Royal Tar* afire in the waters of Penobscot Bay. *Internet Archive Book Images, Wikimedia Commons.*

peeked through a crack in the door and saw the handler with his arm on Mogul's leg, trying to calm the elephant as men dashed about the deck. Maybe the girl, not fully understanding the situation but motivated by a desire to help, slipped through the door to comfort one of the horses.

The *Royal Tar* was now at anchor in the choppy waters of Penobscot Bay, about a mile and a half off Vinalhaven in the Fox Island Thoroughfare. There were ninety-three passengers and crew, a circus menagerie, and a red-hot boiler on board. Some reports suggest that the force pump, a potential auxiliary supply of water, was used at this point to try to bring more water into the boiler. Other reports indicate that the first call of "Fire!" echoed across the boat shortly after the anchor splashed into the bay. Either way, efforts to put out the flames with the pump hoses didn't work. The ceiling above the now red-hot boiler was on fire, including those extra supports added in Saint John to support Mogul's additional weight. And the fire spread. And spread.

The passengers were finally alerted to the situation. The crew had managed to keep the danger from them while all efforts were made to deal with the emergency. It was suggested by a few that if the passengers had known sooner, perhaps some of the men, experienced seamen themselves, could have helped put out the fire or come up with a plan sooner. Or if there had been someone to man the engine pump and get water on the fire or direct the panicked people, perhaps more lives could have been saved. But hindsight is always the bittersweet luxury that only survivors are afforded. And the sad truth is that not all on board that day were able to reflect on what should have or could have happened.

The boiler was in the middle section of the boat, so the deadly flames were contained there initially. Sensing this, passengers ran for the bow and the stern, trying to find an escape from the growing flames. The noise was deafening. Crew members shouted orders. Mothers called out to their children, screaming their names as the smoke and heat increased. Panicked horses reared on their tethers, narrowly missing small children in the melee. Mogul trumpeted wildly as the caged animals below deck—the lionesses and tiger—screamed in horror as the flames got closer and closer.

Captain Reed shouted over the uproar. He called out, "Throw the wagons over. They'll float—and those poles and ropes. Man the buckets, men, and get a chain on that elephant. Hoist the distress flag. Get that longboat overboard!" He called to hoist the sails and raise the anchor. His initial reaction was to make a run for shore, knowing that the passengers' chances of survival would be greater the closer they were to land. However, as soon as the sails were unfurled, a stiff breeze fanned the flames, turning the sails to ash almost immediately. The *Royal Tar* was doomed—a flaming vessel adrift in Penobscot Bay, slowly being carried out to sea. Desperation gripped the crew and passengers, knowing their chances of rescue were slipping away with every passing moment.

Despite the owners and crew being fully aware of the perils of sea travel, by today's standards, the ship was grossly underprepared for an emergency. It had originally been equipped with four lifeboats, but two of these had been left behind in Saint John to make room for the circus animals and wagons, leaving only two on board. These remaining lifeboats, even under the best circumstances, could accommodate no more than thirty people—barely a third of those on board. The stark reality was that these rescue options were woefully insufficient, offering slim chances of survival should disaster strike.

Yet as inadequate as they were, these lifeboats represented the only hope for escape. The passengers and crew knew that they had to try, despite the overwhelming odds. The thought of cramming as many people as possible into these small boats and then casting off into the cold, unforgiving waters was terrifying, but the alternative—staying aboard a ship that was burning around them—was even worse. The situation underscored the harsh realities of maritime travel during this era, when safety measures were often inadequate and the thin line between life and death depended on the whims of the sea.

At the stern, Captain Reed and two crew members lowered the smaller boat, hoping to build rafts in the water to save others. Meanwhile, a crew member and fifteen other men loaded into the larger of the two lifeboats. With oars in place, they rowed off toward shore, never looking back. Their escape, driven by a desperate instinct for self-preservation, meant abandoning the rest of the passengers and crew to their fate. The choice those sixteen people made had severe implications. Captain Reed was now left with only the smaller boat to save over seventy people from the flames rapidly consuming the *Royal Tar*. The remaining passengers, witnessing the larger lifeboat's departure, were gripped by fear and despair, their chances of survival dwindling dramatically. The escape of those sixteen men not only reduced the means of escape but also shattered the morale of those still on board. The growing dangers forced Captain Reed to make quick and crucial decisions, his leadership becoming the last hope for those trapped by the encroaching flames.

Panicked and increasingly desperate, passengers began leaping into the frigid waters of Penobscot Bay to escape the heat and flames. The limbs of many who jumped overboard seized up, succumbing to the cold of the October waters, and they drowned without taking a stroke to save themselves. Passengers threw their steamer trunks and other belongings overboard, hoping that these would be recovered at some later time. One passenger, a man, stuffed all his money into the pockets of his jacket and pants and grabbed a trunk before leaping into the choppy ocean. He was so weighed down by the heavy coins that he sank beneath the waves, never to reappear.

Others jumped into the water and stayed afloat. Captain Reed, in the smaller remaining lifeboat, was near the *Royal Tar*. He and the others helped pull several people from the waters. One of them was J.T. Sherwood, the British consul at Portland. Another was James H. Fowler of Saint John. These were a few of the passengers specifically identified and who later gave reports on the events of the day.

Help was on the way. The distress flag Reed raised, or perhaps the flames themselves, were spotted by the U.S. revenue cutter *Veto*, stationed in Castine, Maine. Located only four to five miles away and under the command of Captain Howland Dyer, the *Veto* reached the site of the *Royal Tar* about half an hour after the fire started. The *Veto* was a schooner and not nearly as large as the *Royal Tar*, so her rescue boats were quite small and not very useful. Captain Dyer faced a difficult dilemma: he was hesitant to bring his ship too close to the inferno, as the *Veto* was carrying munitions, including gunpowder. Concerned that the gunpowder might explode, he kept what he deemed to be a safe distance.

The crew of the *Veto*, anxious to help, watched the blazing ship with a mix of fear and frustration. They could see the frantic passengers and crew of the *Royal Tar*, and the cries for help echoed across the water. Some crew members suggested throwing the gunpowder overboard to safely approach the burning vessel, but Captain Dyer decided caution was necessary, knowing the risk of an explosion was too great to ignore. Later, passengers would reflect on whether offloading the gunpowder might have allowed for a more impactful rescue effort. However, Captain Dyer's decision, made in the heat of the moment, was driven by a need to protect his crew and vessel. Once again, hindsight makes all decisions made in a time of crisis seem straightforward and easy.

Captain Reed began to row toward the *Veto* as she became visible in the distance. Some of the men onboard refused to help, saying that it was fruitless, as they were rowing a small boat against the wind. Captain Reed proclaimed, "I was captain of the big boat and damn me if I will not be captain of the small one; and if any man refuses to run for the cutter, I'll throw him overboard!"

To some passengers onboard, it appeared that Captain Reed was rowing away from the boat, abandoning them to their fate. Panic, disbelief, and fear spread among them as they watched him disappear into the distance, seemingly just as those other sixteen men had done. While it was true that he did row away, his intention was not to leave them behind. Captain Reed was making his way to a safer distance to assess the situation and plan a rescue. He returned multiple times to rescue passengers, each time facing the growing intensity of the flames and the desperation of those begging for rescue.

The situation became more ominous by the minute. The fire was concentrated, for the moment, in the center of the boat. Passengers, therefore, crowded at either the bow or the stern, unable to pass between them. Families became separated and isolated, with parents torn from their children. People on one end of the boat could not see or hear those at the other end. Fear and confusion were palpable, spreading like the flames consuming their boat. The passengers didn't know the fate of the others. Faces turned pale, eyes wide with terror, as people clutched each other, desperate to stay together. Shouts and cries filled the air, a mix of panic and confusion. Passengers prayed aloud, their voices trembling, while others screamed for help, their fear consuming them. Survivors told stories of desperation and heroism and the tragedies they witnessed. Some told of a young girl, perhaps an older sister, who pushed two small children into the water off the stern. They managed to swim to a hay bale floating in the bay, likely intended for the animals. Captain Reed eventually picked them up in his lifeboat. The older girl did not survive.

The crew sprang into action with grim determination, their movements quick and purposeful despite the chaos. Some crew members formed a bucket brigade, desperately dousing the flames with seawater, their faces streaked with soot and sweat. Others tried to maintain order among the panicked passengers, shouting for calm and guiding people away from the most dangerous areas.

In the turmoil, some of the animals broke free from their restraints, racing around the deck in terror. The horses, eyes wide with fear and nostrils flaring, galloped in frantic circles, their hooves clattering against the wooden deck. The camels, normally placid and slow, were now in sheer panic, their long legs flailing as they stumbled and bellowed. Mogul, the elephant, trumpeted loudly, swinging his trunk in distress and turning the scene into a frenzy of pandemonium. The once orderly deck became a battleground of terrified animals and desperate humans, the uproar of panicked cries and thundering hooves overwhelming the senses and escalating the already dire situation.

According to one report, Mogul found his way to the part of the boat where the flames were not raging. He stood on his hind feet with his front feet poised on the railing. To passengers, it looked as if Mogul was weighing his options, not sure what to do. He stayed there until about 4:00 p.m., nearly an hour and a half after the fire started.

With no other options, a few of the animal handlers from the menagerie, their faces etched with worry, pushed the horses and two camels into the water, hoping they might swim to safety. The animals began to circle the boat in endless, frantic loops. Under less stressful conditions, these animals could easily swim the distance to shore. But now, confused and frightened, they swam around and around the boat, clearly terrified. The horses' manes became matted with seawater, and the camels' humps bobbed up and down as they paddled aimlessly. Exhaustion overtook them. One by one, they sank beneath the waves, their desperate struggles coming to a tragic end. The cries of both passengers and animals filled the air, amplifying the sense of terror that hung over the scene as the *Royal Tar* helplessly drifted further from safety.

With the two lifeboats gone, passengers were desperate on board. Some tried to throw the menagerie's omnibus overboard, thinking it might float and serve as a lifeboat for many. But it proved to be too heavy, and even the strength of many men was not enough to accomplish this.

It was a horrifying nightmare; no words were able to accurately describe the extreme choices people faced. Women threw their babies into the bay and then jumped in after them. Weighted down by their heavy dresses and petticoats, many drowned at sea. Some tied the ropes dangling along the sides of the boat around their waists and lowered themselves into the cold October waters, still tied to the boat. As the fire spread, those ropes were burned, separating from the boat and sending the people adrift, with heavy ropes tied around their bodies. One woman swam around the boat twice, looking for help, but drowned before she was rescued.

As the *Royal Tar* burned, the passengers were thrust into an inconceivable nightmare, surrounded by chaos and destruction. A fierce gale whipped through the rigging, creating choppy seas that tossed the ship and scattered debris far and wide. The fire raged uncontrollably, sending flaming timbers and burning fragments of sail crashing down around them, while thick smoke choked the air, making it difficult to see or breathe. The intense heat from the flames was matched only by the biting cold of the October waters below.

The sea around the burning ship became a chaotic, nightmarish landscape, further intensified by the relentless gale. The churning waters were filled with debris—charred fragments of the ship's timbers, trunks, and personal belongings hastily thrown overboard and burning pieces of sail that whipped through the air like fiery projectiles. Amid this wreckage, people struggled against the violent waves, their cries for help barely audible over the roar of the wind and the crackling of the flames.

The passengers faced a horrifying choice between staying aboard the burning ship or plunging into the frigid, unforgiving sea. Flaming debris and collapsing masts turned the deck into a deadly obstacle course, while the cold waters below sapped the strength and hope of those who jumped or were thrown overboard. In this maelstrom, survivors desperately tried to construct makeshift rafts from the floating debris. They clung to anything that might keep them afloat—splintered wood, overturned trunks, even pieces of the burning sail—but the debris, caught in the swirling winds and heaving waves, made survival seem almost impossible.

The scene was a brutal testament to the overwhelming power of nature and the fragility of life in the face of such unforgiving forces. The noise was deafening—the roaring wind, the crackling fire, and the chaotic sounds of people and animals fighting for their lives. Every moment was a battle for survival, with the passengers and crew facing overwhelming odds in their desperate fight against the elements.

One person who worked to save himself by tying himself to one of the ropes was Henry H. Fuller of the menagerie. He had been in his cabin at the time the fire started, sick from the motion of the seas over the past few days. He described the horror and chaos on the boat: "The screams of women and children, the horrid yells of the men, the roaring of the storm, and the awful confusion baffle description."

Fuller was unsure which avenue to take to save himself. Unable to get into a lifeboat, and unwilling to jump in the water, he sat on the edge of the boat, at the railing at the stern, until his coat caught fire. He quickly tamped down the flames and checked around. As far as he could tell from his perspective at the stern, there was no one else aboard. There may have been others at the bow, but the fire had cut the two ends of the boat off from each other, and neither knew what was happening on the other side.

Fuller later described his experience. He "fastened a rope to the tiller chain and dropped over the stern, where I found about fifteen others hanging in different places, mostly in the water. In fact, the water washed over us almost every minute."

Imagine for a moment the scene. Exhausted horses swam in circles around the ship, adrift in choppy seas, fire consuming the center part. People jumped into the water while others crowded onto the boat, clinging to ropes, chains, and any part of the vessel they could grasp to keep themselves from the cold, dark waters of Penobscot Bay. Some of the cages burst open, releasing serpents and snakes onto the deck. Chased by flames, they slithered into any corner they could find to escape. Parrots, with their vibrant feathers now singed and darkened, fluttered desperately, unable to find a safe perch. The once orderly menagerie had turned into a scene of utter pandemonium, with animals and humans alike fighting for survival in the midst of the inferno. Fuller had said it best: the scene baffled all description.

Fuller's description continues:

> *While holding on, I saw several drown; some were beaten from their hold by the waves, and some falling into the sea for want of strength to sustain themselves any longer. I had fastened my rope to the chain, which was again fastened by iron bolts, which held out against the fire much longer than the other parts, to which many were suspended. I wound the rope around my*

> *neck and thigh; and was enabled to bear up the additional weight of three men and a lady, who hung securely to me.*

According to his account in *The Conflagration of the Steamer Royal Tar*, Fuller was not the only passenger clinging to the boat, attached by ropes or chains, holding others up. Near him, Atkins, the pilot of the *Royal Tar*, was holding fast to the boat. Atkins, a seasoned mariner with a weathered face, had faced many challenges in his years at sea, but this was undoubtedly the bleakest. As he hung on desperately for his life, he searched the faces of those around him for his son, the one who had discovered the low boiler. Through the chaos, a woman hanging onto a nearby rope could hold on no longer. Her arms, drained of strength and trembling from the exertion, gave out, and she let go.

Fuller watched in awe and fear as Atkins somehow managed to grab her as she fell, using his legs to hold her between them as they dangled above the water. His face, contorted with effort, betrayed the sheer willpower it took to keep her from plunging into the sea.

Suddenly, a wave tossed the woman around, causing her to slip free again. She fell into another man whom Fuller identified as an Irishman. The Irishman, determined and strong, managed to catch her just in time. His accent was thick as he shouted encouragement, adding a touch of humanity to the grim scene. Fuller, Atkins, and the Irishman all encouraged the woman to hold on, their voices rising above the tumultuous waves. With their support, she managed to cling to the boat once more. The dreadful situation underscored their desperation as they fought to survive, each moment a battle against the merciless waves and their own exhaustion. The woman, driven by fear and willpower, clung to the lifeline provided by these brave men. Together, they formed a fragile chain of survival, each one's fate intertwined as the *Royal Tar* continued her struggle against the unforgiving sea.

Other passengers clung to debris or ropes hanging from the bow of the boat. A few people began fashioning a makeshift raft from the wreckage, hoping to stay afloat until they could be rescued. As they were hoisting themselves out of the water, they heard a loud crash above them, rising above the already-deafening noise of the ship. They must have looked up to see Mogul finally making the choice to leap into the ocean to save himself. The circus elephant landed on the raft, drowning all those on board. An article in the November 11, 1836, edition of the *Hillsborough Times* reported that after jumping into the ocean, Mogul turned around and communicated with his handler, waving his trunk in the air, signaling for him to jump into the water, too. What happened to the handler is unknown, but Mogul was last seen swimming away from the boat.

Another passenger, Captain Waite of Portland, hung onto a rope dangling off the end of the boat. As the rope burned, he managed to swim around to the boat's rudder and get his arm through the chain there, supporting himself, along with a woman who held onto his hand and a man who dangled from his leg. They clung to the chain for an hour and a half before being rescued.

W.H. Harrison, the twenty-four-year-old who had spent the summer building a bridge over the Saint John River and was on his way to visit friends, found himself in the water, struggling to keep his head above the waves. He tried, unsuccessfully, to make a raft out of the debris. Still, he swam to the stern to get as far from the flames as he could. There, he found several other people, including Captain Waite, clinging to ropes and each other. Harrison and First Mate Alex Black of Pugwash, Nova Scotia, clung to the *Royal Tar* for what they estimated was about three hours. The *Royal Tar*, still ablaze, drifted out to sea with Black and Harrison hanging onto the stern. The sun set early on that stormy late October day, and it was almost dark when Black and Harrison drifted close enough to an island to swim to safety.

Captain Reed rowed passengers he rescued from the water to the *Veto*. He said afterward, "When I returned for another load [of people] the steamer was a sheet of flame. Most of the remaining passengers had jumped into the water and were hanging to the ropes which hung over the side of the vessel. Some of the ropes burned in two and the persons holding them were drowned before we could rescue them."

The *Royal Tar* continued to drift out to sea, flames still raging. There were no more people to save. Captain Reed had reached all who could be reached. The lives, hopes, dreams, and futures of thirty-three souls were lost that day. Beloved animals, brought from far across the world, shared the same fate in the cold, dark waters off the coast of Maine. The sea claimed not only human lives but also the majestic creatures that had once captivated so many, their stories culminating in a tragic, united end.

Survivors huddled and shivered on the *Veto*, watching the *Royal Tar* burn. Captain Reed, head low and shoulders drooped in defeat, slowly rowed back to the *Veto*, the weight of the deaths of those he could not save hanging heavily over him. Witnesses watched, numb, as a lone woman wailed in fear and grief at the bow of the boat as the flames crept closer. She had just seen her child and sister succumb to the waves of Penobscot Bay. The flames blocked her final moments from the witnesses, so it is uncertain if she succumbed to the flames or the waves, but she was the last victim of the tragedy that unfolded that October day off the coast of Maine.

Exhaustion set in among the survivors as the frantic energy of the rescue gave way to the crushing weight of reality. They were drenched and shivering, their faces etched with shock and horror. The knowledge that nothing more could be done settled on them like iron chains, each person grappling with the enormity of the tragedy they had just witnessed. The future held the daunting task of figuring out what had happened. Two major questions hung in the air: How did the fire start? Could it have been prevented? The responsibility of uncovering the truth loomed large, adding another layer of burden to already weary shoulders. There was an unspoken agreement among the survivors that answers were needed, not just for themselves but for those who had been lost.

The *Royal Tar*, consumed by fire and swallowed by the sea, left behind a legacy of sorrow. Its story, one of tragedy and resilience, would be told and retold, a somber reminder of the fragility of life and the unpredictable nature of fate. As the survivors looked out over the dark waters, the weight of what had happened pressed down on them. They made a silent vow to never forget the souls lost that day.

CHAPTER 6

WHAT CAME NEXT

Onlookers watched as the *Royal Tar*, now a fiery ruin, was pushed out to sea by the howling winds. The last flicker of flames was seen around ten o'clock that night near Isle au Haut, and then it vanished into the darkness. The flames finally disappeared from view, swallowed by the horizon as the *Royal Tar* slipped beneath the waves. The survivors, huddled together on the *Veto*, watched in stunned silence as the reality of what had just unfolded settled in. Their faces were etched with exhaustion, their minds grappling with the enormity of the tragedy they had narrowly escaped. The cries and chaos of the day were replaced by an eerie calm, a stark contrast to the storm of emotions brewing within.

As the sun dipped lower, casting long shadows across the water, a heavy sense of finality hung in the air. But with that finality came the inevitable questions—what had gone wrong, who was to blame, and how would they move forward? The events of that day would be dissected and debated, stories retold and examined from every angle. Heroes had been born from the flames, their courage shining through in moments of unimaginable terror. But cowards, too, were made, their choices in those desperate hours leaving a shadow that would linger. The thin line between life and death had been drawn by fate, choices, and circumstance, shaping the futures of those who survived and sealing the loss of those who did not.

This was the moment before the storm, the deep breath before the chaos of inquiry and accountability began. The headlines that would soon sweep across the region were already being penned, setting the stage for

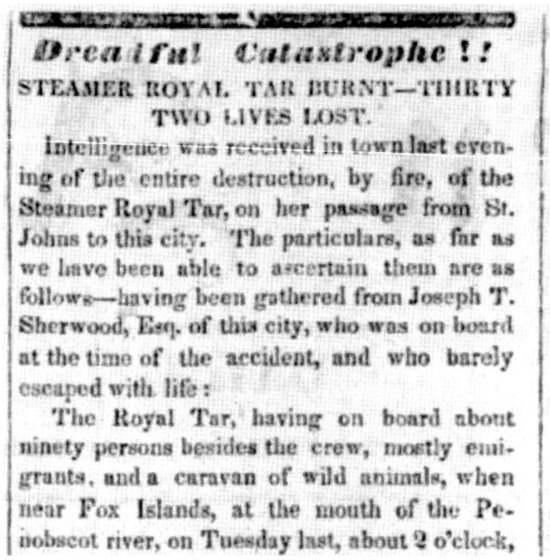

Dreadful Catastrophe!!

STEAMER ROYAL TAR BURNT—THIRTY TWO LIVES LOST.

Intelligence was received in town last evening of the entire destruction, by fire, of the Steamer Royal Tar, on her passage from St. Johns to this city. The particulars, as far as we have been able to ascertain them are as follows—having been gathered from Joseph T. Sherwood, Esq. of this city, who was on board at the time of the accident, and who barely escaped with life:

The Royal Tar, having on board about ninety persons besides the crew, mostly emigrants, and a caravan of wild animals, when near Fox Islands, at the mouth of the Penobscot river, on Tuesday last, about 2 o'clock,

SPIRIT OF THE MAILS.

PARTICULARS OF THE LOSS OF THE STEAMBOAT ROYAL TAR.

The Portland Advertiser brings us the particulars of the dreadful accident which occurred on board this boat on the 25th inst. They differ on some respects from the account published on Saturday, but still our correspondent was as accurate as under the circumstances of haste and confusion could have been expected.

ISLE HOLT, 25th October.

Dear Sir,—I am sorry to inform you of the loss of the Royal Tar, by fire yesterday about two o'clock, crossing Penobscot Bay, about two miles from the Fox Islands The fireman had let the steam down by some accident, and we

Left: In the days that followed, newspapers across New England began to write about the disaster. Portland Press Herald, *October 29, 1836.*

Right: Captain Reed's letter to the owners of the *Royal Tar* made the newspaper as editors raced to bring the latest news to their readers. Bangor Daily Whig and Courier, *October 31, 1836.*

the aftermath that would follow. And as the first waves of grief began to crash against the survivors, they knew that what came next would be just as malevolent as the fire that had consumed their ship.

A COMMUNITY JOINS TOGETHER

The *Veto* brought the passengers Captain Reed had rescued to nearby Kimball's Harbor on Isle Haut (now referred to as Isle au Haut). Locals from the island and nearby areas rushed to help the stunned and shivering survivors. One passenger specifically mentioned the kindness of those who assisted them:

- Miss S. Crocket, who brought shoes and other necessities to the female survivors
- The Thomas brothers, who were "notably kind"
- Captain Dyer of the *Veto*, who not only took aboard the passengers rescued by Captain Reed but also took the injured female passengers to his home to provide bandages and first aid
- Mr. Allen, who worked at a marble works facility and helped arrange stagecoach passage for the women to Portland

The tragic loss of life on that fateful day was profound. In total, at least thirty-three people perished, their lives claimed by the unforgiving waters of Penobscot Bay or the merciless flames aboard the *Royal Tar*. Most of the victims drowned, pulled under by the cold, churning sea, but reports indicated that one woman met an even more horrifying fate. Mary Watts, the stewardess, was the only known person to have burned to death, trapped in the inferno as the ship was engulfed by flames. Her death stands as a stark reminder of the desperate situation aboard the *Royal Tar*, where escape routes were few.

Tragically, among the dead were an estimated six to eight children and infants whose presence was not recorded on Captain Reed's manifest. Their absence from the official record, and the fact that none survived, suggests that the true death toll may have been even higher. The loss of these young lives adds a particularly poignant layer to the disaster, as families were torn apart in the chaos and the youngest, most vulnerable passengers had no chance against the elements.

Despite the devastation, a glimmer of humanity shone through in the actions of William Barter, a fisherman from Isle au Haut. He is credited by the New England Historical Society with rescuing some of the survivors. Barter brought them back to his home, where his wife welcomed them with warmth and kindness, settling them into soft feather beds after serving a hearty meal of hasty pudding, lamb, baked beans, and freshly baked bread. This act of compassion provided a brief respite for those who had endured unbelievable terror, a moment of comfort in the midst of overwhelming loss.

The disaster also brought with it significant financial devastation. Aboard the *Royal Tar* was an estimated $60,000 worth of specie and paper money, a sum equivalent to about $2 million today. This included not only the profits from the circus's successful summer tour but also the personal belongings and savings of the passengers. When combined with the loss of the ship and the baggage it carried, the total monetary loss was estimated at $120,000 (nearly $4 million in today's currency). The *Royal Tar* was a total loss. In the days following the disaster, only a single steamer trunk was found floating in the waters, containing $90, or $3,000 in today's terms. A schooner that arrived in Portland on November 12 reported passing the charred remains of a burned ship near Cash's Ledge, but nothing else was ever recovered. The wreck of the *Royal Tar*, along with the lives and fortunes it carried, disappeared into the depths, leaving behind only memories and a few scattered remnants of a once-grand voyage.

Captain Reed

The *Bangor Daily Whig and Courier* published the letter Captain Reed sent to the owners of the *Royal Tar* in its October 31 edition. He began his letter with:

> *Dear Sir,—I am sorry to inform you of the loss of the* Royal Tar, *by fire yesterday about two o'clock, crossing Penobscot Bay, about two miles from the Fox Islands. The fireman had let the steam down by some accident, and we were obliged to anchor. After about half an hour at anchor, we found her on fire under the deck and over the boiler. We instantly set our force pump at work with the hose, but the men could not stand at the pump for the smoke. By this time, the flames were coming up the hatch of the Engine Room, and there was no hope of putting it out. We took to the boats, two in number. I got possession of one, and some passengers of the other, 16 of them in number—and they pulled from us and made the best of their way for the shore.*

Reed stated pointedly, "I have no blame to attach to anybody as regards the fire—I think it was pure accident." With this statement, Captain Reed set the tone for the investigation into the disaster, clearly asserting that the fire was accidental.

Reed also subtly suggested that the owners had a responsibility to those on board: "We expect to get a schooner tomorrow and send the passengers on in her. You will please forward the deck passengers to Boston free of expense, for they have lost all they had—as well as everybody else. I saved nothing, not even my money. There was no time to think of anything but life."

The owners had not insured the *Royal Tar*, so it is unclear how they compensated the passengers, but it seems likely they paid out of their own pockets. Reed continued, "I intend going back to St John at the first opportunity with the crew that are saved, which are all hands except two men and one woman, stewardess."

Reed closed his somber letter with this reflection:

> *Had our fire engine been on deck we could have put the fire out easily. It is a great oversight having a fire engine to work below. I have nothing particular to write further. I do not feel like writing or anything else. I am very stiff from overexertion, but hope to be better shortly. The people here have been very kind indeed, and we are as well off as can be expected. I remain your most obedient, Thomas Reed.*

Little has changed along Market Wharf since Captain Reed took his daily walks there as harbor master. *Provincial Archives of New Brunswick and author's collection.*

Humble to the end, that was Captain Reed. Reed and the crew did make their way back to Saint John the following Saturday aboard the schooner *Ploughboy*, out of Eastport. Captain Reed was met at the dock with more grave news. In the time since he had left just a few days before, his son, William, had contracted an illness and died. The youngster, age eighteen, died on October 25, the same day his father rescued forty people from a burning ship. The newspaper article in Saint John read: "Died, on Tuesday morning, after a short illness, William Grant, son of Captain Thomas Reed, in the 18th year of his age. Funeral on Saturday at 2 o'clock, from his father's residence, when the friends and acquaintances of the family are requested to attend."

Captain Reed is buried, along with his wife, in what is now Fernhill Cemetery in Saint John, New Brunswick. *Author's collection.*

When the *Royal Tar* set off on October 21, William was in good health and spirits, bidding his father goodbye at the dock. A short illness, possibly cholera, struck him, and he died after forty-eight hours. His death coincided with his father's rescue efforts, and he was buried a few hours after his father returned home.

The *New Brunswick Courier* published an article on October 31, 1836, in which Captain Reed expressed his gratitude:

> *Thomas Reed, Master of the late steamer* Royal Tar, *begs to tender his sincere thanks to Captain Howland Dyer, commanding the United States Cutter* Veto, *and his crew, for their great exertions in saving the survivors from the steamer when on fire in Penobscot Bay on the 25th October. He also extends his gratitude to Capt. William Baker, Capt. George Kimball, Capt. William Yeaton, Mr. Nathan Sawyer, Mr. Samuel Turner, Mr. Eben Sawyer, and Mr. William Staples, all inhabitants of the Isle of Haut, for their humane attention to the sufferers.*

Captain Reed was awarded a purse of $621 a month later, in appreciation and recognition of his bravery and command on that day. He became captain of a new steamer, the *Nova Scotia*, in 1838. This boat made trips between Saint John and Eastport. He returned to Saint John, where he was made harbormaster of the port in 1841.

He was often seen walking the streets along the wharf in Saint John, accompanied by his loyal dog. Captain Reed died on August 28, 1860. He is buried in Fernhill Cemetery in Saint John in a quiet, older part of the stately cemetery.

Eyewitness Accounts

The overwhelming sentiment was that Captain Reed was a hero. His bravery and determination resulted in his saving numerous lives that stormy day. While research shows some detractors made their opinions on the tragedy known, they were few and far between. The *Camden Herald* published a story about the *Royal Tar* on January 11, 1895, in which two men who witnessed the disaster as teenagers provided their accounts.

Captain Kent, who was about fifteen years old in 1836, lived on the island of North Haven near the Fox Island Thoroughfare. He watched the disaster unfold from a hill on his family's property, seeing the *Royal Tar* drift out to sea until it burned out. Captain Calderwood, also fifteen at the time, was working on his grandfather's farm on Vinalhaven and saw, from that distance, the *Royal Tar* become consumed in flames. Both men suggested that from their vantage points and experiences as teenagers, "The terrible loss of life might have been avoided had the vessel remained at anchor and the longboat remained by to take the passengers to shore, which was so near, or had the captain instead of anchoring run the steamer ashore." They were undoubtedly correct, and Captain Reed did try those tactics and might have been successful had the sails not caught fire. Many agree that the actions of the sixteen men who took the longboat and disappeared may have cost lives.

In an interview with the *Camden Herald* on January 11, 1895, Captain Kent discussed how the scene he witnessed that day had stayed with him for years. He said, "I can see the masts of that steamer falling over her side as plainly today as I saw them then." That memory haunted him for nearly sixty years.

Some surviving passengers told a reporter with the *Eastport Sentinel* a few days after the wreck that the "disastrous event was occasioned by gross and unpardonable negligence on the part of the second Engineer, who was on duty."

THE SIXTEEN WHO LEFT

And what about those sixteen men who commandeered one of the lifeboats and rowed off, never to return? Many consider them cowards, selfish men who abandoned their fellow passengers and crew members. Numerous sources refer to them as such. However, it is worth noting that these men were never publicly identified and did not face any charges after the investigation into the disaster. One source generously suggested that perhaps their escape was more practical than nefarious and that with the stormy sea conditions, it may have been next to impossible for them to maneuver the largest lifeboat back to the ship to rescue others. Perhaps they tried and failed. The truth, along with the lives of thirty-three people and the circus animals, was forever lost that day.

CAPTAIN DYER

Captain Dyer of the *Veto* was later severely injured in a cannon explosion in Castine Harbor. He survived and served as the keeper of Brown's Head Light on Fox Island, a position he held for many years.

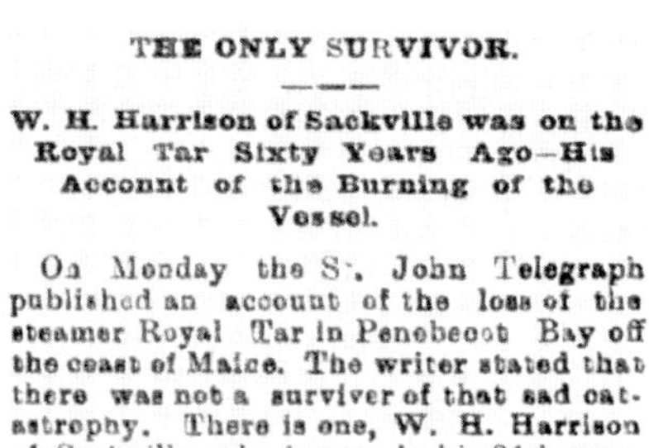

THE ONLY SURVIVOR.

W. H. Harrison of Sackville was on the Royal Tar Sixty Years Ago—His Account of the Burning of the Vessel.

On Monday the St. John Telegraph published an account of the loss of the steamer Royal Tar in Penobscot Bay off the coast of Maine. The writer stated that there was not a surviver of that sad catastrophy. There is one, W. H. Harrison of Sackville, who is now in his 84th year.

Even decades later, the story of the *Royal Tar* captured the imaginations of locals. An interview with W.H. Harrison made headlines. The details from his interview are included in the pages of this book. The Evening Mail, *October 30, 1896*.

SURVIVORS GATHER

For years after the disaster, the men of Saint John who survived would meet for lunch on October 25 of each year. They would commemorate the event, trade memories, and enjoy each other's company. Harrison and George Eaton were two of the last survivors to do so. Harrison died on October 20, 1886, just days before the fiftieth anniversary.

The Replacement Ship

As tragic as the wreck of the *Royal Tar* was, life had to go on. The route between Saint John and Portland, Maine, had proved to be very popular, and there was still a need for a boat to fill that route. Early in 1837, the steamship *Gazelle* replaced the *Royal Tar*. The *Gazelle*, not long after, crashed against the rocks on shore and was a complete loss. Thankfully, all passengers and crew were rescued, unscathed.

The Circus Animals

It is presumed that all, or at least most, of the animals traveling with Fuller's Menagerie and Burgess's collection of serpents and birds perished in the fire aboard the *Royal Tar*. However, for years after the disaster, there were persistent reports of sightings of exotic animals up and down the islands of Penobscot Bay, suggesting that some may have met a different fate. Among these stories, locals spoke of a population of unusual snakes that were said to have taken up residence on Crotch Island, south of Deer Isle. These snakes, believed to be remnants of the circus, became a part of the island's folklore, their presence a reminder of the tragedy that had unfolded at sea.

There were also rumors of larger animals that might have made it to shore. One such tale involved a tiger, allegedly spotted prowling the woods near a local farm. The story goes that the tiger was eventually shot by a farmer, possibly because it had begun preying on his livestock. The idea of a tiger stalking the forests of coastal Maine captured the imaginations of many, blending the boundary between fact and legend. Some reports also suggested that two of the horses from the menagerie had survived and made it to shore, though their ultimate fate remains unclear.

Mogul, the elephant that had been a star attraction of the circus, became the subject of much speculation. Some claimed that he had made it to Brimstone Island, where he was housed in a barn by a sympathetic farmer. Others, however, were less optimistic, believing that Mogul had perished along with the other animals. His fate, like so much about the disaster, remains shrouded in mystery, leaving behind only whispers and conjecture among the islanders.

AS WORD SPREAD

When the news of the fire aboard the *Royal Tar* reached Saint John, the city was gripped by a wave of shock and sorrow. Just days earlier, the people of Saint John had marveled at the circus animals, watching in awe as they paraded through the streets and boarded the ship. The vivid memories of those exotic creatures and the excitement they had brought to the town now stood in stark contrast to the tragic news of their demise. The city's atmosphere was thick with sadness, and concern for loved ones who had been aboard the ill-fated vessel spread through the community like wildfire.

One poignant story that emerged from this tragedy was that of Mrs. A.T. Small of Stonington. As a small child, she had waved at an elderly woman aboard the *Royal Tar* as it sailed past. When she heard the news of the fire, her heart sank, and she anxiously scoured the lists of survivors, hoping against hope to find the woman's name. But none of the survivors were elderly women, and Small realized with a heavy heart that the woman she had seen, who had so warmly acknowledged her wave, had likely perished in the flames or the frigid waters.

This realization left young Small with a deep sense of grief, yet she found a small measure of comfort in recalling the woman's actions. As the ship passed, the old woman had appeared to whisper a prayer, perhaps a final plea to God. In that memory, Small found a sliver of hope—believing that the woman's faith had carried her through those final moments, offering a semblance of peace amid the terror. The story of their brief connection, a fleeting moment of humanity in the face of such overwhelming loss, remained with Small throughout her life, serving as a testament to the enduring impact of the *Royal Tar* tragedy on all who were touched by it.

A THING OF POETRY

In 1837, a book of two poems by Arthur Slader called *The Conflagrations* was published. Slader, a local poet of some renown from Saint John, wrote a poem about the *Royal Tar* shortly after the accident called "The Burning Boat: A serio-satiric poem on the destruction by fire of the Steamer *Royal Tar* (of Saint John, N.B.) in Penobscot Bay, on the 25th October, 1836." He added a descriptive poem called "The Burning City" to commemorate the fire that ravaged the city of Saint John on January 14, 1837.

THE BURNING BOAT:

A SERIO-SATIRIC POEM ON THE DESTRUCTION BY FIRE OF THE STEAMER

ROYAL TAR,

(OF SAINT JOHN, N. B.)

IN PENOBSCOT BAY, ON THE 25TH OCTOBER,

1836.

The poem "The Burning Boat" was one of two fire-themed poems in Slader's book. *Arthur Slader, 1837.*

Slader's poems are long and descriptive. One passage from "The Burning Boat" reads: "'Twas post-meridian, and not far from three—'Fire!' was the cry—(How that terrific sound Appals us, even though on shore we be!) Both fore and aft those horrid cries resound, Commingling with the murmurs of the sea: While all above, and all below—around—Was frantic uproar—clasmours confusion, If you've a heart 'will quiver at th'asllusion."

Another less respectful and introspective rhyme circulated through Saint John in the aftermath of the *Royal Tar* tragedy. This verse, which had the tone of a children's rhyme—something you might hear chanted over a game of jump rope—quickly spread through the town. The words were even written on a piece of canvas and posted on the Hopley Theater, not far from the wharf where the *Royal Tar* had departed on its ill-fated voyage. The rhyme read, in part:

> *The* Royal Tar, *she went too far,*
> *Her boiler got too hot;*
> *She'll never see St. John again,*
> *Because she's gone to pot.*

Though this jingle was catchy, it was also regrettably irreverent. The fact that it made its way into the annals of time is unfortunate, as it fails to respect the gravity of the tragedy that claimed so many lives. Nonetheless, the rhyme's simplicity and rhythm ensured its place in local memory, a reminder of how quickly even the most solemn events can be reduced to a few flippant lines in popular culture.

The "Ghost" of the Royal Tar

The story of the *Royal Tar* became a legend in Saint John and Penobscot Bay. Almost four decades later, in 1876, locals on Fox Island and the surrounding areas of Isle au Haut, Deer Isle, and others noticed a strange, eerie glow at night in the waters off Fox Island. The flame hovered just above the ocean's surface, and as people watched, they became convinced it was moving like a ship adrift in stormy seas. Old fishermen on Vinalhaven confidently said, "It's the ghost of the *Royal Tar*." This conviction spread, convincing hundreds on the surrounding islands.

Adding to the mystique, superstitious old women spoke of hearing the cries of women and children, the panicked roars of lions, and the trumpeting of an elephant faintly echoing from the direction of the glow.

Reverend G.W. Avery of Ellsworth Falls, Maine, sat down with Henry Buxton, a feature writer for the *Bangor News*, years later to share his story of the legend of the *Royal Tar*. Avery was seventeen years old, the son of a stonecutter and a student at Vinalhaven High School. That year, the eerie glow off the coast and the superstitious whispering of the locals sent the island into what Avery called a "frenzy of superstition." It seemed everyone on the island believed there was a ghost ship in Penobscot Bay. People flocked to a hill at the edge of town at night to watch the ghostly light until it faded into the darkness. Teenage boys would take their girlfriends to the hill to watch, whispering ghost stories to frighten them and then offering comfort.

Avery said, "It was a bigger thrill than the movies of today." He had seen the lights himself and wasn't scared. Though he didn't believe in ghosts, he was very curious. Always up for a schoolboy adventure, Avery convinced a couple of friends to investigate the phenomenon with him. One of them had a small yawl, so they used that to row a few miles from shore to where the lights were seen. Avery described what happened next: "We rested on our oars for a while, watching, and then suddenly, about 2,000 yards from us, appeared the light—a great big flame which seemed to come right out of the water. A spooky sight indeed." Avery and his friends likened it to a will-o'-the-wisp in a swamp. They rowed furiously after the light, but it kept eluding them. It was eerie, but none of the boys suggested giving up. They were hell-bent on chasing down the ghost of the *Royal Tar*.

The light would suddenly disappear, as if a dark blanket had been thrown over it, only to reappear farther away. It was as if the spirits at work knew they were being pursued. They continued their chase until 2:00 a.m., when they were close to the shore of Isle au Haut. The next light they saw was from the cottage of a fisherman on the coast of Isle au Haut. Hungry after hours of chasing the light, they knocked on the fisherman's door and were rewarded with warm doughnuts and glasses of cold milk.

As the boys devoured the doughnuts, they listened to the fisherman talk about his night of "torching for herring." Avery and the others paused, realizing the fisherman's method explained the mysterious light. The fisherman described how he attached a sheet iron contraption resembling a huge frying pan with a cover to the stern of his dory. In the pan, a fierce fire of pine knots burned. To attract the herring to the surface, he would pull the lid, and the water in the wake of the boat would become brilliantly illuminated by the flame. While the lid was off, he would row like mad, and when he had attracted enough herring, he would drop his oars, grab his net, and scoop in the fish. Then down would go the lid, and the flame would disappear.

The boys realized they had been chasing a herring fisherman around Penobscot Bay, not the ghost of the *Royal Tar*. The legend had grown from an old-fashioned fishing method into a ghost story. The boys vowed never to speak of their foolishness or spoil the fun for others who believed. Avery finished his story by saying, "I have kept that a secret until this very minute when I am telling it to you."

A view of the cold, gray waters of the Penobscot Bay from Owl's Head Lighthouse, near Rockland, Maine. The final resting place of the *Royal Tar* is a few miles out from here. *Author's collection.*

THE *ROYAL TAR* NOW rests beneath the waters of Penobscot Bay, its final resting place marked on maps but hidden from view, a silent witness to the tragedy that unfolded on that fateful day.

The calm waters that now cover the site are a stark contrast to the chaos and flames that once consumed the ship. In the quiet of the bay, where the waves gently lap against the shore, there is a sense of peace, a reminder that time, like the sea, moves on. Yet beneath the surface, the memory of those lost lingers, etched in the hearts of those who survived and in the history of the region. As you gaze at the serene waters, it's impossible not to feel both the weight of sorrow and a flicker of hope—a hope that, even in the face of such loss, we can find meaning and resilience in the stories we tell and the memories we keep.

CHAPTER 7

A STORY THAT DOES NOT END

A shipwreck in 1836—that has to be relegated to the dusty, unread annals of history, right? Not exactly. The story of the *Royal Tar* has a remarkable way of resurfacing in modern times, keeping its legacy alive nearly two hundred years later.

Music and Art

- In 1999, the Maine-based folk trio Schooner Fare released a song called "The *Royal Tar*" on their album *Our Maine Songs*. This lively sea shanty provides a largely accurate account of the tragedy. As the chorus explains: "'There's a fire!' someone shouted, 'Fire in the hole!' And a northwest wind across the deck to chill the very soul. Their courage would be tested 'ere that fateful night was through. Of cowards there were many, of heroes just a few."
- Maine artist Annie Bailey was featured in the annual BASH at the Farnsworth Art Museum group, the [Collective], on April 1, 2016. The theme of the art show was "An April Fools Circus," and Bailey's contribution focused on the story of the *Royal Tar*. She submitted a hand-drawn animation of the events in the form of a crankie. Crankies are an old form

of storytelling where a sequential painting moves through a box, using a crank, to tell a story. The result is like that of an old silent movie. Bailey's work, created on a roll of vellum and painted with India ink, was thirty-five feet in length. She begins with the steamship and shows the animals loading onto the *Royal Tar* in Saint John and the crowds and passengers waving goodbye. Her art can be found on YouTube.

ADVENTURE

The waters in Penobscot Bay in the Fox Island Thoroughfare are between twenty and forty feet deep, certainly within reach of someone with scuba gear. Although the conditions are often poor in this area, it is surprising that no one has searched extensively for the wreckage of the *Royal Tar*. The specie was never recovered, and it is estimated that a significant amount of treasure was on board. There would likely be valuable and interesting artifacts from the circus as well. A video from Sub Sea Research Production, posted on YouTube in 2014, discusses the wreck of the *Royal Tar* and the possibility of searching for the missing specie.

LITERATURE

- Maine children's book author Chris Van Dusen wrote *The Circus Ship* in 2009. Inspired by the real-life events that occurred on the *Royal Tar*, Van Dusen wrote and illustrated a wonderful story about animals that swam ashore to an island in Maine after their steamship sank. With a much happier ending than the real story, Van Dusen's book is a heart-warming homage to the actual tragedy.
- Maine author Mark Warner published *The Tragedy of the Royal Tar* in 2010. His book served as a starting point for much of the research in this book.
- Poet Robert Cording published a poem called "The Horses" in the *New England Review* published by Middlebury College Publications. The poem begins with a description on which

it is based: "In the 19th century the steamer, *Royal Tar*, sunk off the coast of Matinicus Island. It was carrying a circus on board."

Podcasts

The award-winning weekly podcast *New England Legends*, written and cohosted by Jeff Belanger, covered the *Royal Tar* in Episode 145. On May 28, 2020, Belanger and cohost Ray Auger traveled to Vinalhaven to reminisce about the circus and the wreck in their episode "The Wreck of the *Royal Tar*."

Beer

Sebago Brewing Company, based in Gorham, Maine, brews year-round, seasonal, and small-batch beers, sometimes with a Maine theme. One of their limited-release brews is an imperial stout called Royal Tar. Inspired by the events of October 25, 1836, this stout is a delicious and refreshing way to honor the infamous steamship.

The Royal Tar Imperial Stout is made by the Sebago Brewing Company in celebration and remembrance of the ship that sank in the waters of Penobscot Bay. *Sebago Brewing Company.*

COFFEE

44 North Coffee, sellers of coffee roasted in Deer Isle, Maine, also honors the story with a special Royal Tar Blend. Their website offers the three-bean blend dedicated to the story of the *Royal Tar* circus ship.

THIS IS A STORY that does not end. From music and art to literature, podcasts, and even beer, the legacy of the *Royal Tar* continues to inspire and intrigue, proving that some tales are too compelling to be forgotten.

EPILOGUE

MOGUL, OCTOBER 25, 1836

It is assumed that all the animals, including Mogul, perished that stormy late October afternoon. Several witness accounts describe Mogul, our majestic elephant, jumping overboard to escape the heat of the flames, inadvertently destroying a makeshift raft built by passengers. He was last seen swimming away from the shore, and it is widely believed that he drowned in those choppy waters, far from his home.

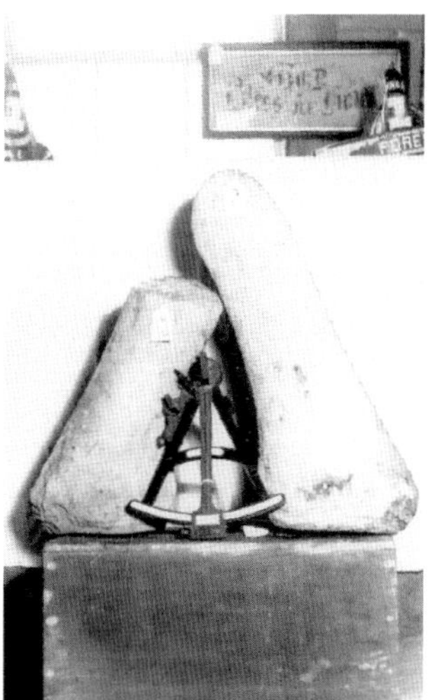

A grainy photograph of two large bones that washed up on the shores of Vinalhaven. To some, they look remarkably similar to the bones of an elephant. *Courtesy of the Vinalhaven Historical Society.*

But perhaps this is not the whole story. Maybe Mogul met a different fate. A photograph surfaced showing what might be elephant bones washed ashore on Vinalhaven. While some believe they are whale bones, just as many, if not more, think they are elephant bones. The bones seem to be from the foot or lower leg of a large animal like an elephant. The only recorded account of an elephant in the waters of Penobscot Bay is Mogul from the *Royal Tar*. Maybe these are his bones? No more bones were found, leaving the whereabouts of the rest of his body a mystery. Some reports mentioned a large carcass washing up on Brimstone Island, southeast of Vinalhaven, a few weeks after the disaster. However, there is no conclusive evidence of this, only speculation based on long-ago conversations and stories.

An article provided by the Vinalhaven Historical Society suggests an answer to the mystery of Mogul's fate. It states: "As no particular mention is made of the elephant, from which our big bone is said to have come, we infer that in the scramble that must have taken place, he may have lost one of his hoofs, but he evidently saved his trunk and started for Europe."

So maybe, just maybe, Mogul survived. Elephants are excellent swimmers, and perhaps Mogul, free of his chains and missing part of one leg, swam off into the open ocean, trunk lifted optimistically into the air, having survived the sinking of the *Royal Tar*.

IN MEMORY OF THOSE LOST ON THE *ROYAL TAR*

Mary Canton
Peggy Cochlan
Charles Curtain, wife, and child
Mr. A. Curtis
Mary Donogh
Mary Hickey
Eliza Hogan
John Hogan
Mary (Margaret) Hogan and child
Thomas Mahoney
Mary Martin
Dennis O'Brien
Fanny (Martin) O'Brien
Mr. J. Price of Saint John, New Brunswick
Mr. J. Ryan and his son, William, from Halifax, Nova Scotia
Mr. S. Siller of Boston, formerly a member of the orchestra at the Tremont Theater
Matty Smith and child
Nicholas Thrembail
Approximately eight other children

Crew Lost

John Day, seaman (or deck officer)
Charles Ford, seaman
Margaret Watts (also referred to as Margaret Burr), stewardess

REFERENCES

Books

Ellms, Charles. *The Tragedy of the Seas; or Sorrow on the Ocean, Lake, and River, from Shipwreck, Plague, Fire, and Famine*. W.A. Leary, 1848.

Howland, S.A. *Steamboat Disasters and Railroad Accidents in the United States: To Which Is Appended Accounts of Recent Shipwrecks, Fires at Sea, Thrilling Incidents, etc*. Dorr, Howland, 1840.

Standiford, Les. *Battle for the Big Top*. Hachette Book Group, 2021.

Thayer, Stuart. *American Circus Anthology: Essays of the Early Years*. 2005.

———. *Traveling Showmen: The American Circus Before the Civil War*. Astley & Ricketts Limited, 1997.

Van Dusen, Chris. *The Circus Ship*. Candlewick Press, 2009.

Warner, Mark. *The Tragedy of the Royal Tar*. Down East Books, 2010.

Weber, Susan, Kenneth L. Ames, and Matthew Wittman, eds. *The American Circus*. Bard Graduate Center, 2012.

Journal Articles

Cording, Robert. "The Horses." *New England Review* 4, no. 1 (1981): 21–33.

Reynolds, W.K. "The Loss of the Royal Tar." *The New Brunswick Magazine* 1 (1898): 45–60.

Newspaper and Magazine Articles

American Traveler. "Visits to the Menagerie." March 27, 1835.

Bangor Daily Whig and Courier, November 2, 1836.

Boston Courier, November 1, 1836.
Boston Patriot. "Just Received." May 13, 1831.
Camden Herald. "Burning of the Royal Tar." January 11, 1895.
The Evening Mail. "The Only Survivor." October 30, 1896.
Evening Transcript (Boston), October 31, 1836.
Hillsborough (FL) Times. "Loss of the British Steam Boat Royal Tar." November 11, 1836.
Mason, John. "The Wreck of the 'Royal Tar.'" *Yankee Magazine*, October 1965.
Newburyport Herald. "The Elephant Mogul." February 24, 1835.
Portland Maine Argus. Scrapbook 120. Accessed at the Maine Historical Society.
Yarmouth Herald. "Great Attraction." August 19, 1836.

Websites

Boat Trader. "Boating Superstitions." www.boattrader.com/research/boating-superstitions.
Official Data. "Inflation Calculator." www.officialdata.org.
Provincial Archives of New Brunswick. "Passenger Lists." Provincial Archives of New Brunswick. archives.gnb.ca/Irish/Databases/PassengerLists/default.aspx?culture=en-CA.
Teach Us History. "Teaching History." www.teachushistory.org.
Yachting News. "Boating Superstitions." www.yachtingnews.com/boating-superstitions.

INDEX

ABOUT THE AUTHOR

Jane Parks Gardner is the author of numerous STEM-focused books and study guides for K–12 learners and adults.

Throughout her extensive and varied career, Jane has embraced many roles, including chemistry professor, high school teacher, editor, author, curriculum developer, world traveler, adventurer, tea drinker, skilled procrastinator, and mom. She is thrilled to add "chronicler of the *Royal Tar*" to her list of accomplishments.

In researching this book, Jane embarked on a journey to New Brunswick and Maine, tracing the route of the *Royal Tar*. She explored the steep streets of Saint John and gazed out at the docks at Peter's Wharf. Traveling down the coast, she stopped in Eastport, where the *Royal Tar* spent several days, and continued to Owl's Head Lighthouse, where she looked out at Penobscot Bay at the waters off Vinalhaven where the ship met its fiery end. Many of the photos in this book were taken during this trip, reflecting her belief in experiencing her stories firsthand.

Jane Parks Gardner resides in Massachusetts.